Acts of Resistance

Acts of Resistance

Against the Tyranny
of the Market

Pierre Bourdieu

translated from the French
by Richard Nice

The New Press
New York

First published in France as Contre-feux by Editions Liber-Raisons d'Agir.
Published in the United Kingdom by Polity Press in association with
Blackwell Publishers Ltd.

ISBN 1-56584-523-4

Published in the United States by The New Press, New York
Distributed by W. W. Norton & Company, Inc., New York

The New Press was established in 1990 as a not-for-profit alternative to the
large, commercial publishing houses currently dominating the book publishing industry. The New Press operates in the public interest rather than for
private gain, and is committed to publishing, in innovative ways, works of
educational, cultural, and community value that are often deemed insuffi-
ciently profitable.

www.thenewpress.com

Printed in the United States

9   8   7   6   5   4   3   2   1

Contents

To the Reader

The texts that follow were written or spoken as contributions to movements and moments of resistance, and it is because I believe that the dangers that provoked them are neither isolated nor occasional that I decided to bring them together for publication. Although they are more exposed than methodically controlled texts to the inconsistencies stemming from the diversity of circumstances, I hope that they can still provide useful weapons to all those who are striving to resist the scourge of neo-liberalism.[1]

I do not have much inclination for prophetic interventions and I have always been wary of occasions in which the situation or a sense of solidarity could lead me to overstep the limits of my competence. So I would not have engaged in public position-taking if I had not, each time, had the – perhaps illusory – sense of being forced into it by a kind of legitimate rage, sometimes close to something like a sense of duty.

The ideal of the collective intellectual, to which I have tried to conform whenever I could make common cause with others on some particular point, is not always easy to put into effect.[2] And if, to be effective, I have sometimes had to commit myself

in my own person and my own name, I have always done it in
the hope – if not of triggering a mobilization, or even one of
those debates without object or subject which arise periodically
in the world of the media – at least of breaking the appearance
of unanimity which is the greater part of the symbolic force of
the dominant discourse.

Notes

1 At the risk of increasing the number of breaks in tone and style
   resulting from the diversity of situations, I have presented
   this selection of articles and contributions here in their
   chronological order, so as to make clearer the historical
   context of remarks which, though they are not reducible to
   a given context, make no concessions to the vague and wordy
   generalities of what is sometimes called 'political philosophy'.
   I have added here and there some basic references to enable
   the reader to explore further the argument that is put
   forward.
2 From all my collective interventions, in particular those of the
   Association de Réflexion sur les Enseignements Supérieurs et
   la Recherche (ARESER), the Comité International de Soutien
   aux Intellectuels Algériens (CISA) and the International
   Parliament of Writers (with which I no longer feel affinities),
   I have chosen only the article published in *Libération*, here
   entitled 'The status of foreigners: a shibboleth', with the
   agreement of my co-authors, both visible (Jean-Pierre Alaux)
   and invisible (Christophe Daadouch, Marc-Antoine Lévy and
   Danièle Lochak), victims of the censorship quite spontan-
   eously and routinely exercised by the journalists responsible
   for the so-called *tribunes libres* in the newspapers. Always in

pursuit of the symbolic capital associated with certain names,
they do not like articles signed with the name of a group, or
bearing several names – this is one of the obstacles, and a
significant one, to the constitution of a collective intellectual
– and they tend to remove the names they do not recognize,
either after negotiation or, as happened there, without
consultation.

The Left Hand and the Right Hand of the State

Q   A recent issue of the journal that you edit was devoted to the theme of suffering.[1] It includes several interviews with people whose voices are not much heard in the media: young people on deprived estates, small farmers, social workers. The head-teacher of a secondary school in difficulty, for example, expresses his bitterness. Instead of overseeing the transmission of knowledge, he has become, against his will, the superintendent of a kind of police station. Do you think that individual and anecdotal testimonies of that kind can cast light on a collective malaise?

PB   In the survey we are conducting on social suffering, we encounter many people who, like that head-teacher, are caught in the contradictions of the social world, which are experienced in the form of personal dramas. I could also cite the project leader, responsible for coordinating all the work on a 'difficult estate' in a small town in northern France. He is faced with contradictions which are the extreme case of those currently

Interview with R. P. Droit and T. Ferenczi, published in *Le Monde*, 14 Jan. 1992.

experienced by all those who are called 'social workers': family counsellors, youth leaders, rank-and-file magistrates, and also, increasingly, secondary and primary teachers. They constitute what I call the left hand of the state, the set of agents of the so-called spending ministries which are the trace, within the state, of the social struggles of the past. They are opposed to the right hand of the state, the technocrats of the Ministry of Finance, the public and private banks and the ministerial *cabinets*. A number of social struggles that we are now seeing (and will see) express the revolt of the minor state nobility against the senior state nobility.[2]

Q   How do you explain that exasperation, those forms of despair and those revolts?

PB   I think that the left hand of the state has the sense that the right hand no longer knows, or, worse, no longer really wants to know what the left hand does. In any case, it does not want to pay for it. One of the main reasons for all these people's despair is that the state has withdrawn, or is withdrawing, from a number of sectors of social life for which it was previously responsible: social housing, public service broadcasting, schools, hospitals, etc., which is all the more stupefying and scandalous, in some of these areas at least, because it was done by a Socialist government, which might at least be expected to be the guarantor of public service as an open service available to all, without distinction . . . What is described as a crisis of politics, anti-parliamentarianism, is in reality despair at the failure of the state as the guardian of the public interest.

If the Socialists had simply not been as socialist as they claimed, that would not shock anyone – times are hard and there is not much room for manoeuvre. But what is more surprising is that they should have done so much to undermine the public interest, first by their deeds, with all kinds of measures and policies (I will only mention the media . . .) aimed at liquidating the gains of the welfare state, and above all, perhaps, in their words, with the eulogy of private enterprise (as if one could only be enterprising within an enterprise) and the encouragement of private interest. All that is somewhat shocking, especially for those who are sent into the front line to perform so-called 'social' work to compensate for the most flagrant inadequacies of the logic of the market, without being given the means to really do their job. How could they not have the sense of being constantly undermined or betrayed?

It should have been clear a long time ago that their revolt goes far beyond questions of salary, even if the salary granted is an unequivocal index of the value placed on the work and the corresponding workers. Contempt for a job is shown first of all in the more or less derisory remuneration it is given.

Q   Do you think that the politicians' room for manoeuvre is really so limited?

PB   It is no doubt less limited than they would have us think. And in any case there remains one area where governments have considerable scope: that of the symbolic. Exemplary behaviour ought to be *de rigueur* for all state personnel, especially when they claim to belong to a tradition of commitment to the interests of the least advantaged. But it is difficult not to have doubts when one sees not only examples of corruption (sometimes quasi-official, with the bonuses given to some senior civil servants) or betrayal of public service (that word is no doubt too strong – I am thinking of *pantouflage*[3]) and all the forms of misappropriation, for private purposes, of public property, profits or services – nepotism, cronyism (our leaders have many 'personal friends' . . . [4]), clientelism . . .

And I have not even mentioned symbolic profits! Television has probably contributed as much as bribery to the degradation of civic virtue. It has invited and projected on to the political and intellectual stage a set of self-promoting personalities concerned above all to get themselves noticed and admired, in total contradiction with the values of unspectacular devotion to the collective interest which once characterized the civil servant or the activist. It is the same self-serving attention seeking (often at the expense of rivals) which explains why 'headline grabbing'[5] has become such a common practice. For many ministers, it seems, a measure is only valid if it can be announced and regarded as achieved as soon as it has been made public. In short, large-scale corruption which causes a scandal when it is uncovered because it reveals the gap between professed virtues and real behaviour is simply the extreme case of all the ordinary little 'weaknesses', the flaunting of luxury and the avid acceptance of material or symbolic privileges.

Q   Faced with the situation you describe, how, in your view, do the citizens react?

PB   I was recently reading an article by a German author on ancient Egypt. He shows how, in a period of crisis of confidence in the state and in the public good, two tendencies emerged: among the rulers, corruption, linked to the decline in respect for the public interest; and, among those they dominated, personal religiosity, associated with despair concerning temporal remedies. In the same way, one has the sense now that citizens, feeling themselves ejected from the state (which, in the end, asks of them no more than obligatory material contributions, and certainly no commitment, no enthusiasm), reject the state, treating it as an alien power to be used so far as they can to serve their own interests.

Q   You referred to the considerable scope that governments have in the symbolic domain. This is not just a matter of setting an example of good behaviour. It is also about words, ideals that can mobilize people. How do you explain the current vacuum?

PB   There has been much talk of the silence of the intellectuals. What strikes me is the silence of the politicians. They are terribly short of ideals that can mobilize people. This is probably because the professionalization of politics and the conditions required of those who want to make a career in the parties increasingly exclude inspired personalities. And probably also because the definition of political activity has changed with the arrival of a political class that has learned in its schools (of political science) that, to appear serious, or simply to avoid appearing old-fashioned or archaic, it is better to talk of management than self-management, and that they must, at any rate, take on the appearances (that is to say the language) of economic rationality.

Locked in the narrow, short-term economism of the IMF worldview which is also causing havoc, and will continue to do so, in North–South relations, all these half-wise economists fail, of course, to take account of the real costs, in the short and more especially the long term, of the material and psychological wretchedness which is the only certain outcome of their economically legitimate *Realpolitik*: delinquency, crime, alcoholism, road accidents, etc. Here too, the right hand, obsessed by the question of financial equilibrium, knows nothing of the problems of the left hand, confronted with the often very costly social consequences of 'budgetary restrictions'.

Q   Are the values on which the actions and contributions of the state were once founded no longer credible?

PB   The first people to flout them are often the very ones who ought to be their guardians. The Rennes Congress[6] and the amnesty law[7] did more to discredit the Socialists than ten years of anti-socialist campaigning. And a 'turncoat' activist does more harm than ten opponents. But ten years of Socialist government have completed the demolition of belief in the state and the demolition of the welfare state that was started in the 1970s in the name of liberalism. I am thinking in particular of housing policy.[8] The declared aim has been to rescue the petite bourgeoisie from publicly owned housing (and thereby from 'collectivism') and facilitate their move into ownership of a house or apartment. This policy has in a sense succeeded only too well. Its outcome illustrates what I said a moment ago about the social costs of some economies. That policy is probably the major cause of social segregation and consequently of the problems referred to as those of the *'banlieues'*.[9]

Q   So if one wants to define an ideal, it would be a return to the sense of the state and of the public good. You don't share everybody's opinion on this.

PB   Whose opinion is everybody's opinion? The opinion of people who write in the newspapers, intellectuals who advocate the 'minimal state' and who are rather too quick to bury the notion of the public and the public's interest in the public interest . . . We see there a typical example of the effect of shared belief which removes from discussion ideas which are perfectly worth discussing. One would need to analyse the work of the 'new intellectuals', which has created a climate favourable to the withdrawal of the state and, more broadly, to submission to the values of the economy. I'm thinking of what has been called the 'return of individualism', a kind of self-fulfilling prophecy which tends to destroy the philosophical foundations of the welfare state and in particular the notion of collective responsibility (towards industrial accidents, sickness or poverty) which has been a fundamental achievement of social (and sociological) thought. The return to the individual is also what makes it possible to 'blame the victim', who is entirely responsible for his or her own misfortune, and to preach the gospel of self-help, all of this being justified by the endlessly repeated need to reduce costs for companies.

The reaction of retrospective panic provoked by the crisis of 1968, a symbolic revolution which alarmed all the small holders of cultural capital (subsequently reinforced by the unforeseen collapse of the Soviet-style regimes), created conditions favourable to a cultural restoration, the outcome of which has been that 'Sciences-Po thought'[10] has replaced the 'thought of Chairman Mao'. The intellectual world is now the site of a struggle aimed at producing and imposing 'new intellectuals', and therefore a new definition of the intellectual and the intellectual's political role, a new definition of philosophy and the philosopher, henceforward engaged in the vague debates of a political philosophy without technical content, a social science reduced to journalistic commentary for election nights, and uncritical glossing of unscientific opinion polls. Plato had a wonderful word for all these people: *doxosophers*. These 'technicians of opinion who think themselves wise' (I'm translating the triple meaning of the word) pose the problems of politics in the very same terms in which they are posed by businessmen, politicians and political journalists (in other words the very people who can afford to commission surveys . . .).

Q   You have just mentioned Plato. Is the attitude of the sociologist close to that of the philosopher?

PB   The sociologist is opposed to the doxosopher, like the philosopher, in that she questions the things that are self-evident, in particular those that present themselves in the form of questions, her own as much as other people's. This profoundly shocks the doxosopher, who sees a political bias in the refusal to grant the profoundly political submission implied in the unconscious acceptance of *commonplaces*, in Aristotle's sense – notions or theses *with* which people argue, but *over* which they do not argue.

Q   Don't you tend in a sense to put the sociologist in the place of a philosopher-king?

PB   What I defend above all is the possibility and the necessity of the critical intellectual, who is firstly critical of the intellectual *doxa* secreted by the doxosophers. There is no genuine democracy without genuine opposing critical powers. The intellectual is one of those, of the first magnitude. That is why I think that the work of demolishing the critical intellectual, living or dead – Marx, Nietzsche, Sartre, Foucault, and some others who are grouped together under the label Pensée 68[11] – is as dangerous as the demolition of the public interest and that it is part of the same process of restoration.

Of course I would prefer it if intellectuals had all, and always, lived up to the immense historical responsibility they bear and if they had always invested in their actions not only their moral authority but also their intellectual competence – like, to cite just one example, Pierre Vidal-Naquet, who has engaged all his mastery of historical method in a critique of the abuses of history.[12] Having said that, in the words of Karl Kraus, 'between two evils, I refuse to choose the lesser.' While I have little indulgence for 'irresponsible' intellectuals, I have even less respect for the 'intellectuals' of the political-administrative establishment, polymorphous polygraphs who polish their annual essays between two meetings of boards of directors, three publishers' parties and miscellaneous television appearances.

Q   So what role would you want to see for intellectuals, especially in the construction of Europe?

PB   I would like writers, artists, philosophers and scientists to be able make their voice heard directly in all the areas of public life in which they are competent. I think that everyone would have a lot to gain if the logic of intellectual life, that of argument and refutation, were extended to public life. At present, it is often the logic of political life, that of denunciation and slander, 'sloganization' and falsification of the adversary's thought, which extends into intellectual life. It would be a good thing if the 'creators' could fulfil their function of public service and sometimes of public salvation.

Moving to the level of Europe simply means rising to a higher degree of universalization, reaching a new stage on the road to a universal state, which, even in intellectual life, is far from having been achieved. We will certainly not have gained much if eurocentrism is substituted for the wounded nationalisms of the old imperial nations. Now that the great utopias of the nineteenth century have revealed all their perversion, it is urgent to create the conditions for a collective effort to reconstruct a universe of realist ideals, capable of mobilizing people's will without mystifying their consciousness.

Paris, December 1991

Notes

1 *Actes de la Recherche en Sciences Sociales*, 90, Dec. 1991, special issue 'La souffrance'; Bourdieu et al., *La Misère du monde.*

2 Alluding to the author's book *The State Nobility: Elite Schools in the Field of Power* (trans.).

3 The practice whereby civil servants move to positions in the private sector (trans.).

4 François Mitterrand (President of France 1981–1995) was often praised for his '*fidélité en amitié*', and a number of personalities appointed to important posts were, according to the newspapers, chiefly noted for being his 'personal friends' (trans.).

5 *effets d'annonce* in the original, produced when a minister reduces his political action to the ostentatious announcement of spectacular decisions which often have no effect or no follow-up –Jack Lang has been cited as an example (trans.).

6 The Rennes Congress (15–18 March 1990), the scene of heated disputes between the leaders of the major tendencies within the Socialist Party, Lionel Jospin, Laurent Fabius and Michel Rocard (trans.).

7 The amnesty that was granted, in particular, to the generals of the French army in Algeria who attempted a putsch against de Gaulle's government (trans.).

8 See Bourdieu et al., 'L'économie de la maison', *Actes de la Recherche en Sciences Sociales*, 81–2, Mar. 1990.

9 Socially analogous to the 'inner cities' but in France implying peripheral housing estates (trans.).

10 As generated and taught in the institutes of political science ('Sciences-Po'), in particular the one in Paris (trans.).

11 Allusion to Ferry and Renaut, *La Pensée 68* (trans.).

12 Vidal-Naquet, *Les Juifs, la mémoire et le présent.*

Sollers *tel quel*

Sollers *tel quel*, Sollers as such, at last . . .[1] There is a curious Spinozan pleasure of truth revealing itself, necessity being accomplished, in the confession of a title: 'Balladur tel quel', the concentrate, with high symbolic density, almost too sublime to be true, of a whole trajectory: from *Tel Quel* to Balladur,[2] from the fake avant-garde of literature (and politics) to the authentic political rearguard.

Nothing very remarkable about that, some will say – those who know, and have long known, that what Philippe Sollers has thrown at the feet of the presidential candidate, in a gesture unprecedented since the time of Napoleon III, is not literature, still less the avant-garde, but the imitation of literature, and of the avant-garde. But the counterfeit is calculated to take in the audience for whom he intends it, all those the cynical courtier wants to flatter, the Balladurians and the Balladurophile *énarques*,[3] with enough culture from

This text was published in *Libération*, 27 Jan. 1995, following the publication of an article by Philippe Sollers, entitled 'Balladur tel quel', in *L'Express*, 12 Jan. 1995.

Sciences-Po for dissertations in two points and embassy
dinners; and also all the masters of pretence who have clustered
at one time or another around *Tel Quel* – the pretence of being
a writer, or a philosopher, or a linguist, or all of those at once,
without being any of them or knowing anything about all that;
when one 'knows the tune' of culture but not the words, when
one only knows how to *mimic* the gestures of the great writer,
and even, for a while, make terror reign in the world of letters.
Thus, in so far as this unscrupulous Tartuffe of the religion of
art succeeds in his imposture, he mocks, humiliates and
degrades the whole heritage of two centuries of struggle for
autonomy of the literary microcosm by casting it at the feet
of the culturally and politically[4] most abject power; and with
himself he prostitutes all the often heroic authors – Voltaire,
Proust or Joyce – with whom he claims allegiance in his role
as literary correspondent[5] for semi-official magazines and
journals.

The cult of transgression without risk which reduces libertin-
ism to its erotic dimension leads him to make cynicism one of
the Fine Arts. Turning the postmodern principle 'anything
goes' into a rule of life, and claiming the right to say anything
and its opposite, simultaneously or successively, he is able to
have his cake and eat it – to criticize the society of the spectacle
and to play the media personality,[6] to glorify Sade and revere
Pope John Paul II, to make revolutionary pronouncements and
intervene in defence of traditional spelling, to deify the writer
and to murder literature (I am thinking of his novel *Femmes*).

This man who presents and sees himself as an incarnation of
freedom has always floated at the whim of the forces of the field.
Preceded and authorized by all the political slippages of the era
of Mitterrand, who may have been to politics, and more
precisely to socialism, what Sollers has been to literature, and

more precisely to the avant-garde, he has been carried along by all the political and literary illusions and disillusions of the age. And his trajectory, which appears to him as an *exception*,[7] is in fact statistically modal, that is to say banal, and as such is exemplary of the career of the writer without qualities of a period of political and literary *restoration*: he is the ideal-typical incarnation of the individual and collective history of a whole generation of writers of ambition, of all those who, having moved, in less than thirty years, from Maoist or Trotskyist terrorism to positions of power in banks, insurance companies, politics or journalism, will readily grant him their indulgence.

His originality – for there is one – is that he has made himself the theorist of the virtues of recantation and betrayal, and so, in a prodigious self-justificatory reversal, has managed to define all those who refuse to recognize themselves in the new, liberated, 'been there, done that' style as dogmatic, archaic, even terrorist. His countless public interventions are so many exaltations of inconsistency, or, more exactly, of *double inconsistency* – calculated to reinforce the bourgeois vision of artistic revolt – the one which, by a double U-turn, a double half-revolution, leads back to the point of departure, the fluttering sycophancies of the young provincial bourgeois, for whom Mauriac and Aragon wrote prefaces.

Paris, January 1995

Notes

1 Philippe Sollers, French author, founder and editor of the journal *Tel quel* (trans.).
2 Edouard Balladur, conservative politician (RPR), former

prime minister, candidate in the presidential election of 1995 against Jacques Chirac and Lionel Jospin (trans.).

3 Graduates of the École Nationale d'Administration, an elite school training France's top civil servants (trans.).

4 As Prime Minister, Balladur had as his Minister of the Interior Charles Pasqua, the author of a particularly repressive law on immigration (trans.).

5 Philippe Sollers regularly contributes a column of literary criticism in *Le Monde*, part of a circuit of literary mutual admiration (trans.).

6 Sollers is a great admirer of the works of Guy Debord (author of *La Société du spectacle*) and a frequent participant in all kinds of TV programmes (trans.).

7 Sollers is the author of a book entitled *Théorie des exceptions* (trans.).

The Status of Foreigners: a Shibboleth

The question of the status that France gives to foreigners is not a 'detail'. It is a false problem which has regrettably come to the forefront as a terribly ill-formulated central question in the political battle.

The Groupe d'Examen des Programmes Électoraux sur les Étrangers en France (GEPEF), convinced that it was essential to force the constitutional candidates[1] to make their views clear on this issue, has carried out an experiment whose findings deserve to be made known. With the exception of Robert Hue,[2] and of Dominique Voynet,[3] who has made it one of the central themes of her campaign, with the abrogation of the Pasqua laws,[4] the regularization of the status of persons not subject to expulsion and the concern to protect the rights of minorities, the candidates side-stepped the attempt to ask them a set of

This text, published in *Libération*, 3 May 1995, signed by Jean-Pierre Alaux and myself, presents the findings of the survey which the GEPEF carried out in March 1995, in which eight candidates for the presidential election were invited to 'discuss their proposals regarding the situation of foreigners in France', a subject practically absent from the election campaign.

questions. Edouard Balladur sent a letter setting out generalities unrelated to our twenty-six questions. Jacques Chirac did
not respond to our request for an interview. Lionel Jospin
mandated Martine Aubry and Jean-Christophe Cambadélis to
answer for him, but they were as uninformed as they were
uninformative about the positions of their favourite.

You don't need a degree in political science to discover in their
silences and in their discourse that they do not have much to
set against the xenophobic discourse which, for some years now,
has been working to generate hatred out of the misfortunes of
society – unemployment, delinquency, drug abuse, etc. Perhaps
for lack of convictions, perhaps for fear of losing votes by
expressing them, they have ended up no longer talking about
this false problem, which is always present and always absent,
except in conventional stereotypes and more or less shame-faced
innuendoes, with their references for example to 'law and order',
the need to 'reduce entries to the lowest possible level' or to
clamp down on 'clandestine immigration' (with occasional
references, to give a progressive tinge, to 'the role of traffickers
and employers' who exploit it).

All these vote-catching calculations, only encouraged by the
logic of a political and media universe fascinated by opinion
polls, are based on a series of presuppositions which are without
foundation – or with no other foundation in any case than the
most primitive logic of magical participation, contamination by
contact and verbal association. To take one of countless
examples: how can one speak of 'immigrants' to refer to people
who have not 'emigrated' from anywhere and who are moreover
described as 'second-generation'? Similarly, one of the major
functions of the adjective 'clandestine' which fastidious souls
concerned for their progressive image link with the term
'immigrants' is surely to create a verbal and mental identifica-

tion between the undetected crossing of frontiers by people and the necessarily fraudulent and therefore clandestine smuggling of objects that are forbidden (on both sides of the frontier) such as drugs or weapons. This is a criminal confusion which causes the people concerned to be thought of as criminals.

These are beliefs which politicians end up believing to be universally shared by their electors. Their vote-catching demagogy is based on the assumption that 'public opinion' is hostile to 'immigration', to foreigners, to any kind of opening of the frontiers. The verdicts of the 'pollsters' – the modern-day astrologers – and the advice of the spin-doctors who make up for their lack of competence and conviction, urge them to strive to 'win votes from Le Pen'. But, to limit ourselves to just one argument, though a fairly strong one, the very score which Le Pen now obtains, after two years of the Pasqua laws and of language and measures directed towards law and order, suggests that the more the rights of foreigners are reduced, the bigger the electorate of the Front National grows (this is obviously something of a simplification, but no more so than the idea often put forward that any measure aimed at improving the legal status of foreigners on French territory would have the effect of increasing Le Pen's vote). What is certain, in any case, is that before imputing the electoral score of the Front National solely to xenophobia, one should consider some other factors, such as the corruption scandals that have besmirched the medio-political world.

When all that has been said, one still needs to rethink the question of the status of the foreigner in modern democracies, in other words of the frontiers which can legitimately be imposed on the movement of persons in worlds which, like our own, derive so much advantage from the circulation of persons and goods. One should at least, in the short term, if only in the logic of enlightened self-interest, evaluate the costs for the country of the law-and-order policy associated with the name of Mr Pasqua – the costs resulting from discrimination in and through police checks, which can only tend to create or reinforce 'social fracture', and from the increasingly widespread violation of fundamental rights, costs for the prestige of France and its particular tradition as defender of human rights, etc.

The question of the status accorded to foreigners is indeed the decisive criterion, the *shibboleth*[5] enabling one to judge the capacity of the candidates to take a position, in all their choices, against the narrow-minded, regressive, security-minded, protectionist, conservative, xenophobic France, and in favour of the open, progressive, internationalist, universalist France. That is why the choice of the elector-citizens ought to fall on the candidate who most clearly makes a commitment to perform the most radical and most total break with the present policy of France as regards the 'reception' of foreigners. It ought to be Lionel Jospin . . . But will he want it?

Paris, May 1995

Notes

1 *les candidats républicains*, i.e. excluding the overtly racist Front National (trans.).
2 General Secretary of the French Communist Party (trans.).
3 Leader of one of the ecology parties, currently Minister of the Environment in the Jospin government (trans.).
4 Cf. p. 14, note 4 (trans.).
5 Shibboleth, a decisive test by which a person's capacity can be judged.

Abuse of Power by the
Advocates of Reason

[. . .] From deep inside the Islamic countries there comes a very profound question with regard to the false universalism of the West, or what I call the imperialism of the universal.[1] France has been the supreme incarnation of this imperialism, which in this very country has given rise to a national populism, associated for me with the name of Herder. If it is true that one form of universalism is no more than a nationalism which invokes the universal (human rights, etc.) in order to impose itself, then it becomes less easy to write off all fundamentalist reaction against it as reactionary. Scientific rationalism – the rationalism of the mathematical models which inspire the policy of the IMF or the World Bank, that of the law firms, great juridical multinationals which impose the traditions of American law on the whole planet, that of rational-action theories, etc. – is both the expression and the justification of a Western arrogance, which leads people to act as if they had the monopoly of reason and could set themselves up as world policemen, in

Intervention at the public discussion organized by the International Parliament of Writers at the Frankfurt Book Fair, 15 Oct. 1995.

other words as self-appointed holders of the monopoly of legitimate violence, capable of applying the force of arms in the service of universal justice. Terrorist violence, through the irrationalism of the despair which is almost always at its root, refers back to the inert violence of the powers which invoke reason. Economic coercion is often dressed up in juridical reasons. Imperialism drapes itself in the legitimacy of international bodies. And, through the very hypocrisy of the rationalizations intended to mask its double standards, it tends to provoke or justify, among the Arab, South American or African peoples, a very profound revolt against the reason which cannot be separated from the abuses of power which are armed or justified by reason (economic, scientific or any other). These 'irrationalisms' are partly the product of our rationalism, imperialist, invasive and conquering or mediocre, narrow, defensive, regressive and repressive, depending on the place and time. One is still defending reason when one fights those who mask their abuses of power under the appearances of reason or who use the weapons of reason to consolidate or justify an arbitrary empire.

Frankfurt, October 1995

Notes

1 Bourdieu, 'Deux impérialismes de l'universel'.

The Train Driver's Remark

Questioned after the explosion in the second coach of the express metro train he was driving on Tuesday, 17 October, the driver, who according to witnesses had led the evacuation of the passengers with exemplary calm, warned against the temptation to take revenge on the Algerian community. They are, he said simply, 'people like us'.

This extra-ordinary remark, a 'healthy truth of the people', as Pascal would have said, made a sudden break with the utterances of all the ordinary demagogues who, unconsciously or calculatedly, align themselves with the xenophobia or racism they attribute to the people, while helping to produce them; or who use the supposed expectations of those they sometimes call 'simple folk' as an excuse for offering them, as 'good enough for them', the simplistic thoughts they attribute to them; or who appeal to the sanctions of the market (and the advertisers), incarnated in audience ratings or opinion polls and cynically identified with the democratic verdict of the largest number, in order to impose their own vulgarity and abject servility on everyone.

Text published in *Alternatives Algériennes*, Nov. 1995.

This exceptional remark provided the proof that it is possible to resist the violence that is exerted daily, with a clear conscience, on television, on the radio and in the newspapers, through verbal reflexes, stereotyped images and conventional words, and the effect of habituation that it produces, imperceptibly raising, throughout the whole population, the threshold of tolerance of racist insults and contempt, reducing critical defences against pre-logical thought and verbal confusion (between Islam and Islamicism, between Muslim and Islamicist, or between Islamicist and terrorist, for example), insidiously reinforcing all the habits of thought and behaviour inherited from more than a century of colonialism and colonial struggles. Only a detailed analysis of the film of one of the 1,850,000 'identity checks' recently carried out by the police to the great satisfaction of our Minister of the Interior[1] would give some idea of the multitude of subtle humiliations (condescending use of *tu*, body searches in public, etc.) or flagrant injustices and illegalities (assault, forced entry, violation of privacy) inflicted on a significant proportion of the citizens or guests of this country, once renowned for its openness to foreigners; and also give an idea of the indignation, revolt or rage that such behaviour can arouse. Ministerial pronouncements, visibly designed to reassure, or to satisfy the craving for 'law and order', would at once become less reassuring.

That simple remark contained an exhortation by example to combat resolutely all those who, in their desire always to leap to the simplest answer, caricature an ambiguous historical reality in order to reduce it to the reassuring dichotomies of Manichean thought which television, always inclined to confuse a rational dialogue with a wrestling match, has set up as a model. It is infinitely easier to take up a position for or against an idea, a value, a person, an institution or a situation, than to analyse what it truly is, in all its complexity. People are all the quicker to *take sides* on what journalists call a 'problem of society' – the question of the Muslim veil,[2] for example – the more incapable they are of analysing and understanding its meaning, which is often quite contrary to ethnocentric intuition.

Historical realities are always enigmatic and, while appearing to be self-evident, are difficult to decipher; and there is perhaps none which presents these characteristics in a higher degree than Algerian reality. That is why it represents an extraordinary challenge, both for knowledge and for action. This truth-test of all analyses is also and above all a touchstone of all commitments.

In this case more than ever, rigorous analysis of situations and institutions is undoubtedly the best antidote against partial views and against all forms of Manicheism – often associated with the pharisaic indulgences of 'communitarian' thought – which, through the representations they engender and the words in which they are expressed, are often fraught with deadly consequences.

Paris, November 1995

Notes

1 This was Charles Pasqua – cf. p. 14, note 4 (trans.).
2 The wearing of the 'veil' at school aroused strong protests from a number of 'intellectuals' who saw it as a threat to the secular principles of French state schooling (trans.).

Against the Destruction of a Civilization

I have come here to express our support to those who have been fighting for the last three weeks against the destruction of a *civilization*, associated with the existence of public service, the civilization of republican equality of rights, rights to education, to health, culture, research, art, and, above all, work.

I have come here to say that we understand this deep-rooted movement, in other words both the despair and the hopes that are expressed in it, and which we too feel, to say that we do not understand (or that we understand only too well) those who do not understand it, like the philosopher[1] who, in the *Journal du Dimanche* of 10 December, discovers with stupefaction the 'gulf between the rational understanding of the world', incarnated, according to him, by Prime Minister Juppé – he spells it out for us – and 'the deep wishes of the population'.

Remarks at the Gare de Lyon, Paris, during the strikes of December 1995. Pierre Bourdieu spoke, in the name of the intellectuals supporting the strikers, alongside representatives of trade unions (in particular, SUD) and associations (AC!, Droits Devant, etc.) with whom he had been associated in previous campaigns, at a mass meeting at the station. (Trans.)

This opposition between the long-term view of the enlightened 'elite' and the short-term impulses of the populace or its
representatives is typical of reactionary thinking at all times
and in all countries; but it now takes a new form, with the state
nobility, which derives its conviction of its legitimacy from
academic qualifications and from the authority of science,
especially economics. For these new governors by divine right,
not only reason and modernity but also the movement of change
are on the side of the governors – ministers, employers or
'experts'; unreason and archaism, inertia and conservatism are
on the side of the people, the trade unions and critical
intellectuals.

This technocratic certainty is what Juppé expresses when he
declares: 'I want France to be a serious country and a happy
country.' This can be translated as: 'I want serious people, in
other words the elites, the *énarques*, those who know where the
people's happiness lies, to be able to make the people happy,
even despite the people, against their will. For the common
people, blinded by their desires, as the philosopher said, do not
understand their own happiness – and in particular their good
fortune in being governed by men who, like Mr Juppé,
understand their happiness better than they do.' That is how
the technocrats think and that is their notion of democracy.
And, not surprisingly, they do not understand it when the
people, in whose name they claim to govern, have the supreme
ingratitude to go out into the streets and demonstrate against
them.

That state nobility, which preaches the withering away of the
state and the undivided reign of the market and the consumer,
the commercial substitute for the citizen, has kidnapped the
state: it has made the public good a private good, has made the
'public thing', *res publica*, the Republic, its own thing. What is

at stake now is winning back democracy from technocracy. We must put an end to the reign of 'experts' in the style of the World Bank or the IMF, who impose without discussion the verdicts of the new Leviathan, the 'financial markets', and who do not seek to negotiate but to 'explain'; we must break with the new faith in the historical inevitability professed by the theorists of liberalism; we must invent new forms of collective political work capable of taking note of necessities, especially economic ones (that can be the task of the experts), but in order to fight them and, where possible, to neutralize them.

The present crisis is a historical opportunity, for France and no doubt also for all those, ever more numerous, in Europe and throughout the world, who reject this new choice: 'liberalism or barbarism'. The railway workers, postal workers, teachers, civil servants, students and so many others, actively or passively engaged in the movement, have, through their demonstrations and declarations, through the countless rethinkings that they have provoked, which the media cannot put the lid on, raised quite fundamental problems, too important to be left to technocrats as self-satisfied as they are unsatisfactory. How do we restore for each of us an enlightened, reasonable definition of the future of the public services, of health, education, transport and so on, in coordination with those who, in the other countries of Europe, are exposed to the same threats? How do we reinvent the republican school system, rejecting the progressive introduction of a two-track system, symbolized, in higher education, by the split between the faculties and the Grandes Écoles? The same question can be asked about health or transport. How do we struggle against the growing insecurity of employment, threatening all those who work in the public services and leading to all kinds of dependence and submission which are particularly pernicious in cultural activities such as radio, television or journalism, because of the censorship they entail, or even in education?

In the work of reinventing the public services, intellectuals, writers, artists, scientists and others have a decisive role to play. They can first help to break the monopoly of technocratic orthodoxy over the means of diffusion. But they can also commit themselves, in an organized and permanent way, and not only in the occasional encounters in a context of crisis, alongside those who are in a position to exert a real influence on the future of society – the associations and unions, in particular – and help to draw up rigorous analyses and inventive proposals about the major questions which the orthodoxy of the media and politics makes it impossible to raise. I am thinking in particular of the question of the unification of the world economy and the economic and social effects of the new international division of labour, or the question of the supposed iron laws of the financial markets in whose name so many political initiatives are sacrificed, the question of the function of education and culture in economies where information has become one of the most decisive productive forces, and so on.

This programme may seem purely abstract and theoretical. But it is possible to challenge autocratic technocracy without falling into a populism which has too often been a trap for social movements, and which, once again, serves the interest of the technocrats.

What I wanted to express, in any case, perhaps clumsily – and I apologize to those I may have shocked or bored – is a real solidarity with those who are now fighting to change society. I think that the only effective way of fighting against national and international technocracy is by confronting it on its own preferred terrain, in particular that of economics, and putting forward, in place of the abstract and limited knowledge which it regards as enough, a knowledge more respectful of human beings and of the realities which confront them.

Paris, December 1995

Notes

1 This was Paul Ricœur (trans.).

The Myth of 'Globalization' and the European Welfare State

Everywhere we hear it said, all day long – and this is what gives the dominant discourse its strength – that there is nothing to put forward in opposition to the neo-liberal view, that it has succeeded in presenting itself as self-evident, that there is no alternative. If it is taken for granted in this way, this is as a result of a whole labour of symbolic inculcation in which journalists and ordinary citizens participate passively and, above all, a certain number of intellectuals participate actively. Against this permanent, insidious imposition, which produces, through impregnation, a real belief, it seems to me that researchers have a role to play. First they can analyse the production and circulation of this discourse. There have been a growing number of studies, in Britain, the US and France, which describe very precisely the procedures whereby this worldview is produced, disseminated and inculcated. Through a whole series of analyses of texts, the journals in which they were published and which have little by little imposed themselves as legitimate, the characteristics of their authors, the

Address to the Greek trade union confederation (GSEE), in Athens, Oct. 1996.

seminars in which they meet to produce them, etc., they have shown how, in Britain and France, constant work was done, involving intellectuals, journalists and businessmen, to impose as self-evident a neo-liberal view which, essentially, dresses up the most classic presuppositions of conservative thought of all times and all countries in economic rationalizations. I am thinking of a study of the role of the journal *Preuves*, which was financed by the CIA and had some noted French intellectuals on its editorial board, and which, for twenty or twenty-five years – it takes time for something false to become self-evident – tirelessly, and initially against the current, produced ideas which gradually became taken for granted.[1] The same thing happened in Britain, and Thatcherism was not invented by Mrs Thatcher. The ground had been prepared over a long period by groups of intellectuals most of whom wrote columns in the leading newspapers.[2] A possible first contribution by researchers could be to make these analyses more generally available, in a form accessible to all.

The work of inculcation, which began a long time ago, continues now. And so we see articles appearing, as if by a miracle, just a few days apart, in all the French papers, with variations linked to the position of each paper in the spectrum of newspapers, commenting on the miraculous economic situation of the United States or Britain. This kind of symbolic drip-feed to which the press and television news contribute very strongly – to a large extent unconsciously, because most of the people who repeat these claims do so in good faith – produces very profound effects. And as a result, neo-liberalism comes to be seen as an *inevitability*.

A whole set of presuppositions is being imposed as self-evident: it is taken for granted that maximum growth, and therefore productivity and competitiveness, are the ultimate and sole goal of human actions; or that economic forces cannot be resisted. Or again – a presupposition which is the basis of all the presuppositions of economics – a radical separation is made between the economic and the social, which is left to one side, abandoned to sociologists, as a kind of reject. Another important assumption is the language which invades us: we absorb it as soon as we open a newspaper, as soon as we turn on the radio, and it is largely made up of euphemisms. Unfortunately, I don't have any Greek examples to hand, but I think you would find them easily enough. For example, in France, instead of 'the employers [le patronat]' they say 'the vital forces of the nation [les forces vives de la nation]'; a company that fires its workers is 'slimming', with a sporting metaphor (an energetic body has to be thin). To announce that a company is sacking 2,000 people, the commentator will refer to 'Alcatel's bold social plan'. Then there is a whole game with the connotations and associations of words like flexibility, souplesse, deregulation, which tends to imply that the neo-liberal message is a universalist message of liberation.

Against this doxa, one has to try to defend oneself, I believe, by analysing it and trying to understand the mechanisms through which it is produced and imposed. But that is not enough, although it is important, and there are a certain number of empirical observations that can be brought forward to counter it. In the case of France, the state has started to abandon a number of areas of social policy. The consequence is an enormous amount of suffering of all kinds, not only affecting people afflicted by deep poverty. It can been shown, for example, that the problems seen in the suburban estates of the cities stem from a neo-liberal housing policy, implemented in the 1970s (known as 'aid to the person'). It led to a social segregation, with on the one hand the subproletariat, made up to a large extent of immigrants, remaining on the large estates, and on the other hand the secure workers with a regular wage and the petite bourgeoisie, leaving to live in small detached houses which they bought with crippling loans. This social separation was brought about by a political measure.[3]

In the United States, the state is splitting into two, with on the one hand a state which provides social guarantees, but only for the privileged, who are sufficiently well-off to provide themselves with insurance, with guarantees, and a repressive, policing state, for the populace. In California, one of the richest states of the US – once presented by some French sociologists[4] as the paradise of all liberations – and also one of the most conservative, and which has perhaps the most prestigious university in the world, since 1994 the prison budget has been greater than the budget of all the universities together. The blacks in the Chicago ghetto only know the state through the police officer, the judge, the prison warder and the parole officer. We see there a kind of realization of the dream of the dominant class, a state which, as Loïc Wacquant has shown,[5] is increasingly reduced to its policing function.

What we see happening in America and beginning to emerge in Europe is a process of involution. When one studies the rise of the state in the societies in which it developed earliest, such as France and England, one first sees a concentration of physical force and a concentration of economic force – the two go together, you need money to make war, to police the country and so on, and you need a police force to collect money. Next comes a concentration of cultural capital, and then a concentration of authority. As it develops, this state acquires autonomy, becomes partially independent of the dominant social and economic forces. The state bureaucracy starts to be able to inflect the will of the dominant groups, to interpret them and sometimes to inspire policies.

The process of regression of the state shows that resistance to neo-liberal doctrine and policy is that much greater in countries where the state traditions have been strongest. And that is explained by the fact that the state exists in two forms: in objective reality, in the form of a set of institutions such as rules, agencies, offices, etc., and also in people's minds. For example, within the French bureaucracy, when housing finance was being reformed, the welfare ministries fought against the financial ministries to defend the social housing policy. Those civil servants had an interest in defending their ministries and their positions; but they also believed in what they were doing, they were defending their convictions. The state, in every country, is to some extent the trace in reality of social conquests. For example, the Ministry of Labour is a social conquest that has been made a reality, even if, in some circumstances, it can also be an instrument of repression. And the state also exists in the minds of the workers in the form of subjective law ('it's my right', 'they can't do that to me'), attachment to 'established rights' [les acquis sociaux], etc. For example, one of the great differences between France and Britain is that the Thatcherized British discover that they did not resist as much as they might have, to a large extent because the labour contract is a common law contract and not, as in France, an agreement guaranteed by the state. And now, paradoxically, at the very time when the British model is being held up as an example, British workers look to the Continent and find it offers things that their own labour tradition did not, namely the idea of employment law.

The state is an ambiguous reality. It is not adequate to say that it is an instrument in the hands of the ruling class. The state is certainly not completely neutral, completely independent of the dominant forces in society, but the older it is and the greater the social advances it has incorporated, the more autonomous it is. It is a battleground (for example, between the finance ministries and the spending ministries, dealing with social problems). To resist the *involution of the state*, in other words the regression to a penal state concerned with repression and progressively abandoning its social functions of education, health, welfare, and so on, the social movement can find support from those responsible for social policies, who are in charge of organizing aid to the long-term unemployed, and worried about the breakdown of social cohesion, unemployment, etc., and opposed to the finance people who only want to hear about the constraints of 'globalization' and the place of France in the world.

I've used the word 'globalization'. It is a myth in the strong sense of the word, a powerful discourse, an *idée force*, an idea which has social force, which obtains belief. It is the main weapon in the battles against the gains of the welfare state. European workers, we are told, must compete with the least favoured workers of the rest of the world. The workers of Europe are thus offered as a model countries which have no minimum wage, where factory workers work twelve hours a day for a wage which is between a quarter and a fifth of European wages, where there are no trade unions, where there is child labour, and so on. And it is in the name of this model that flexible working, another magic word of neo-liberalism, is imposed, meaning night work, weekend work, irregular working hours, things which have always been part of the employers' dreams. In a general way, neo-liberalism is a very smart and very modern repackaging of the oldest ideas of the oldest capitalists. (Magazines in the US draw up a league table of these macho bosses, ranked, along with their salary, according to the number of people they have had the courage to sack.) It is characteristic of *conservative revolutions*, that in Germany in the 1930s, those of Thatcher, Reagan and others, that they present restorations as revolutions. The present conservative revolution takes an unprecedented form: in contrast to earlier ones, it does not invoke an idealized past, through exaltation of soil and blood, the archaic themes of the old agrarian mythologies. This new kind of conservative revolution appeals to progress, reason and science (economics in this case) to justify the restoration and so tries to write off progressive thought and action as archaic. It sets up as the norm of all practices, and therefore as ideal rules, the real regularities of the economic world abandoned to its own logic, the so-called law of the market. It ratifies and glorifies the reign of what are called the financial markets, in other words the return to a kind of radical capitalism, with no other law than that of maximum profit, an unfettered capitalism without any disguise, but rationalized, pushed to the limit of its economic efficacy by the introduction of modern forms of domination, such as 'business administration', and techniques of manipulation, such as market research and advertising.

If this conservative revolution can deceive people, this is because it seems to retain nothing of the old Black Forest pastoral of the conservative revolutionaries of the 1930s; it is dressed up in all the signs of modernity. After all, it comes from Chicago. Galileo said that the natural world is written in the language of mathematics. The neo-liberal ideologues want us to believe that the economic and social world is structured by equations. It is by arming itself with mathematics (and power over the media) that neo-liberalism has become the supreme form of the conservative sociodicy which started to appear some thirty years ago as 'the end of ideology', or more recently, as 'the end of history'.

To fight against the myth of globalization, which has the function of justifying a restoration, a return to an unrestrained – but rationalized – and cynical capitalism, one has to return to the facts. If we look at the statistics, we see that the competition experienced by European workers is largely intra-European. According to my sources, 70 per cent of the trade of European countries is with other European countries. The emphasis placed on the extra-European threat conceals the fact that the main danger comes from the internal competition of other European countries and is sometimes called 'social dumping': European countries with less social welfare and lower wages can derive a competitive advantage from this, but in so doing they pull down the others, which are forced to abandon their welfare systems in order to resist. This implies that, in order to break out of this spiral, the workers of the advanced countries have an interest in combining with the workers in less developed countries to protect their social gains and to favour their generalization to all European workers. (This is not easy, because of the differences in national traditions, especially in the weight of the unions with respect to the state and in the means of financing welfare.)

But this is not all. There are also all the effects, visible to everyone, of neo-liberal policies. For example, several British studies have shown that Thatcherite policies have resulted in enormous insecurity, a sense of distress, not only among manual workers but also in the middle classes. The same can be seen in the United States, where there is a great rise in the number of insecure, underpaid jobs (which artificially bring down official unemployment rates). The American middle classes, exposed to the threat of suddenly losing their jobs, are feeling a terrible insecurity (which shows that what is important in a job is not only the activity and income it provides, but also the sense of security it gives). In all countries, the proportion of workers with temporary status is growing relative to those with permanent jobs. Increased insecurity and 'flexibility' lead to the loss of the modest advantages (often described as the 'perks' of the 'privileged') which might compensate for low wages, such as long-lasting employment, health insurance and pension rights. Privatization equally leads to the loss of collective gains. For example, in the case of France, three-quarters of newly recruited workers are taken on on a temporary basis, and only a quarter of those three-quarters will become permanent employees. These new recruits naturally tend to be young people. That is why this insecurity mainly afflicts young people, in France – we observed this in our book *La Misère du monde* – and also in Britain, where the distress of young people has reached very high levels, with consequences such as delinquency and other very costly phenomena.

Added to this, at the present time, is the destruction of the economic and social bases of the most precious cultural gains of humanity. The autonomy of the worlds of cultural production with respect to the market, which had grown steadily through the battles and sacrifices of writers, artists and scientists, is increasingly threatened. The reign of 'commerce' and the 'commercial' bears down more strongly every day on literature, particularly through the concentration of publishing, which is more and more subject to the constraints of immediate profit; on literary and artistic criticism, which has been handed over to the most opportunistic servants of the publishers – or of their accomplices, with favour traded for favour; and especially on the cinema (one wonders what will be left in ten years' time of European experimental cinema if nothing is done to provide avant-garde directors with the means of production and perhaps more importantly distribution). Not to mention the social sciences, which are condemned either to subordinate themselves to the directly self-interested sponsorship of corporate or state bureaucracies or wither under the censorship of power (relayed by the opportunists) or money.

While globalization is above all a justificatory myth, there is one case where it is quite real, that of the financial markets. Thanks to the removal of a number of legal restrictions and the development of electronic communications which lead to lower communication costs, we are moving towards a unified financial market – which does not mean a homogeneous market. It is dominated by certain economies, in other words the richest countries, and more especially by the country whose currency is used as an international reserve currency and which therefore enjoys a greater scope within these financial markets. The money market is a field in which the dominant players – in this case the United States – occupy a position such that they can largely define the rules of the game. This unification of the financial markets around a small number of countries holding the dominant position reduces the autonomy of the national financial markets. The French financiers, the Inspectors of Finances, who tell us that we must bow to necessity, forget to tell us that they make themselves the accomplices of that necessity and that, through them, it is the French national state which is abdicating.

In short, globalization is not homogenization; on the contrary, it is the extension of the hold of a small number of dominant nations over the whole set of national financial markets. There follows from this a partial redefinition of the international division of labour, with European workers suffering the consequences, seeing for example the transfer of capital and industries towards low-wage countries. This international capital market tends to reduce the autonomy of the national capital markets, and in particular to prevent nation-states from manipulating exchange rates and interest rates, which are increasingly determined by a power concentrated in the hands of a small number of countries. National authorities are subject to the risk of speculative assaults by agents wielding massive funds, who can provoke a devaluation, with left-wing governments naturally being particularly threatened because they arouse the suspicion of the financial markets (a right-wing government which acts out of line with the ideals of the IMF is in less danger than a left-wing government even if the latter's policy matches the ideals of the IMF). It is the structure of the worldwide field which exerts a structural constraint, and this is what gives the mechanisms an air of inevitability. The policy of a particular state is largely determined by its position in the structure of the distribution of finance capital (which defines the structure of the world economic field).

Faced with these mechanisms, what can one do? The first thing is to reflect on the implicit limits which economic theory accepts. Economic theory, when it assesses the costs of a policy, does not take account of what are called social costs. For example, a housing policy, the one chosen by Giscard d'Estaing when he was Finance Minister in 1970, implied long-term social costs which do not appear as such: twenty years later, who, apart from sociologists, remembers that measure? Who would link a riot in a suburb of Lyon to a political decision of 1970? Crimes go unpunished because people forget. All the critical forces in society need to insist on the inclusion of the social costs of economic decisions in economic calculations. What will this or that policy cost in the long term in lost jobs, suffering, sickness, suicide, alcoholism, drug addiction, domestic violence, etc., all things which cost a great deal, in money, but also in misery? I think that, even if it may appear very cynical, we need to turn its own weapons against the dominant economy, and point out that, in the logic of enlightened self-interest, a strictly economic policy is not necessarily economical – in terms of the insecurity of persons and property, the consequent policing costs, etc. More precisely, there is a need to radically question the economic view which individualizes everything – production as much as justice or health, costs as well as profits – and which forgets that efficiency, which it defines in narrow, abstract terms, tacitly identifying it with financial profitability, clearly depends on the outcomes by which it is measured, financial profitability for shareholders and investors, as at present, or satisfaction of customers and users, and, more generally, satisfaction and well-being of producers, consumers, and, ultimately, the largest possible number. Against this narrow, short-term economics, we need to put forward an *economics of happiness*, which would take note of all the profits, individual and collective, material and symbolic, associated with activity (such as security), and also all the material and symbolic costs associated with inactivity or precarious employment (for example, consumption of medicines: France holds the world record for use of tranquillizers). You cannot cheat with the *law of the conservation of violence*: all violence is paid for, and, for example, the structural violence exerted by the financial markets, in the form of layoffs, loss of security, etc., is matched sooner or later in the form of suicides, crime and delinquency, drug addiction, alcoholism, a whole host of minor and major everyday acts of violence.

At the present time, the critical efforts of intellectuals, trade unions or associations should be applied as a matter of priority against the withering away of the state. The national states are undermined from outside by these financial forces, and they are undermined from inside by those who act as the accomplices of these financial forces, in other words, the financiers, bankers and finance ministry officials. I think that the dominated groups in society have an interest in defending the state, particularly in its social aspect. This defence of the state is not inspired by nationalism. While one can fight against the national state, one has to defend the 'universal' functions it fulfils, which can be fulfilled as well, or better, by a supranational state. If we do not want it to be the Bundesbank, which, through interest rates, governs the financial policies of the various states, should we not fight for the creation of a supranational state, relatively autonomous with respect to international political forces and national political forces and capable of developing the social dimension of the European institutions? For example, measures aimed at reducing the working week would take on their full meaning only if they were taken by a European body and were applicable to all the European nations.

Historically, the state has been a force for rationalization, but one which has been put at the service of the dominant forces. To prevent this being the case, it is not sufficient to denounce the technocrats of Brussels. We need to develop a new internationalism, at least at the regional level of Europe, which could offer an alternative to the regression into nationalism which, as a result of the crisis, threatens all the European countries to some degree. This would imply constructing institutions that are capable of standing up to these forces of the financial market, and introducing – the Germans have a wonderful word for this – a *Regressionsverbot*, a ban on backward movement with respect to social gains at the European level. To achieve this, it is absolutely essential that the trade unions operate at this European level, because that is where the forces they are fighting against are in action. It is therefore necessary to try to create the organizational bases for a genuine critical internationalism capable of really combating neo-liberalism.

Final point: why are the intellectuals so ambiguous in all this? I will not try to enumerate – it would be too long and too cruel – all the forms of surrender or, worse, collaboration. I will simply allude to the debates of the so-called modern or postmodern philosophers, who, when they are not simply content to let things take their course, occupied as they are in their scholastic games, wrap themselves up in a verbal defence of reason and rational dialogue, or, worse, offer a supposedly postmodern but in fact 'radical chic' version of the ideology of the end of ideology, with the condemnation of the great explanatory narratives or the nihilist denunciation of science.

In fact the strength of the neo-liberal ideology is that it is based on a kind of social neo-Darwinism: it is 'the brightest and the best', as they say at Harvard, who come out on top (Becker, winner of the Nobel prize for economics, developed the idea that Darwinism is the basis of the aptitude for rational calculation which he ascribes to economic agents). Behind the globalist vision of the International of the dominant groups, there is a philosophy of competence according to which it is the most competent who govern and who have jobs, which implies that those who do not have jobs are not competent. There are the 'winners' and the 'losers', there is the aristocracy, those I call the state nobility, in other words those people who have all the properties of a nobility in the medieval sense of the word and who owe their authority to education, or, as they see it, to intelligence, seen as a gift from Heaven, whereas we know that in reality it is distributed by society and that inequalities in intelligence are social inequalities. The ideology of competence serves very well to justify an opposition which is rather like that between masters and slaves. On the one hand there are full citizens who have very rare and overpaid capacities and activities, who are able to choose their employer (whereas the others are at best chosen by their employer), who are able to obtain very high incomes on the international labour market, who are, both men and women, overworked (I recently read an excellent British study of these supercharged executive couples who perpetually jet around the world and earn more than they could dream of spending in four lifetimes . . .), and then, on the other side, there is a great mass of people condemned to borderlines jobs or unemployment.

Max Weber said that dominant groups always need a 'theodicy of their own privilege', or more precisely, a sociodicy, in other words a theoretical justification of the fact that they are privileged. Competence is nowadays at the heart of that sociodicy, which is accepted, naturally, by the dominant – it is in their interest – but also by the others.[6] In the suffering of those excluded from work, in the wretchedness of the long-term unemployed, there is something more than there was in the past. The Anglo-American ideology, always somewhat sanctimonious, distinguished the 'undeserving poor', who had brought it upon themselves, from the 'deserving poor', who were judged worthy of charity. Alongside or in place of this ethical justification there is now an intellectual justification. The poor are not just immoral, alcoholic and degenerate, they are stupid, they lack intelligence. A large part of social suffering stems from the poverty of people's relationship to the educational system, which not only shapes social destinies but also the image they have of their destiny (which undoubtedly helps to explain what is called the passivity of the dominated, the difficulty in mobilizing them etc.). Plato had a view of the social world which resembles that of our technocrats, with the philosophers, the guardians, and then the people. This philosophy is inscribed, in implicit form, in the educational system. It is very powerful, and very deeply internalized. Why have we moved from the committed intellectual to the 'uncommitted' intellectual? Partly because intellectuals are holders of cultural capital and, even if they are the dominated among the dominant, they still belong among the dominant. That is one of the foundations of their ambivalence, of their lack of commitment in struggles. They obscurely share this ideology of competence. When they revolt, it is still because, as in Germany in 1933, they think they are not receiving their due in relation to their competence, guaranteed by their qualifications.

Athens, October 1966

Notes

1 Grémion, *Preuves, une revue européenne à Paris*, and *Intelligence de l'anti-communisme*.
2 Dixon, 'Les Evangélistes du Marché'; Pasche and Peters, 'Les premiers pas de la Société du Mont-Pélerin ou les dessous chics du néolibéralisme'.
3 Cf. Bourdieu et al., 'L'économie de la maison', *Actes de la Recherche en Sciences Sociales*, 81–2, Mar. 1990.
4 In particular, Edgar Morin and Jean Baudrillard (trans.).
5 Wacquant, 'De l'État charitable à l'État pénal'.
6 Cf. Bourdieu, 'The racism of intelligence'.

The Thoughts of Chairman Tietmeyer

I don't want to be here to put the cultural icing on the cake.
The breaking of the bonds of social integration which culture
is asked to reconstruct is the direct consequence of a policy, an
economic policy. And sociologists are often asked to repair
economists' breakages. So, instead of merely offering what, in
hospitals, is called palliative treatment, I would like to raise the
question of the doctors' contribution to the disease. For it might
be that to a large extent the social 'diseases' that we deplore are
produced by the often brutal medicine given to those who are
supposed to be being cured.

To do so, having read in the aeroplane which took me from
Athens to Zurich for an interview with the President of the
Bundesbank, who is presented as 'the high priest of the
deutschmark', neither more nor less, and since I am in a centre
renowned for its traditions of literary exegesis, I would like to
perform a kind of hermeneutic analysis of a text which you will
find in full in *Le Monde* of 17 October 1996.

Address given at the Rencontres Culturelles Franco-Allemandes on 'Social
integration as a cultural problem', University of Freiburg, Oct. 1996.

This is what the 'high priest of the deutschmark' says: 'The crucial issue today is to create the conditions favourable to lasting growth, and the confidence of investors. It is therefore necessary to restrain public spending.' In other words – he is more explicit in the following sentences – to bury as quickly as possible the welfare state and its expensive social and cultural policies, so as to reassure investors, who would prefer to take charge of their own cultural investments. I am sure that they all enjoy Romantic music and expressionist paintings and, while I know nothing of the tastes of the President of the Bundesbank, I can well believe that, like the Governor of the Banque de France, Mr Trichet, he reads poetry and sponsors the arts. He goes on: 'It is therefore necessary to restrain public spending and reduce taxation to a level that is acceptable in the long term.' By which he means: reduce the taxation of investors to a level that is acceptable in the long term to these same investors, lest they be discouraged and driven to take their investments elsewhere. Next: 'reform the social welfare system'. In other words, bury the welfare state and its policies of social protection, which undermine the confidence of investors and provoke their legitimate distrust, because they are convinced that their economic entitlements – we speak of social entitlements, we could equally speak of economic entitlements – I mean their capital, are not compatible with the social entitlements of the workers, and that these economic entitlements must obviously be safeguarded at all costs, even if this means destroying the meagre economic and social benefits of the great majority of the citizens of the Europe to come, those who were frequently described in December 1995 as 'feather-bedded' and 'privileged'.

Mr Tietmeyer is convinced that the social entitlements of the investors, I mean their economic entitlements, would not

survive the perpetuation of a social welfare system. And so this
system has to be reformed, and *quickly*, because the economic
entitlements of the investors cannot wait any longer. And to
prove to you that I am not exaggerating, I read further from
the words of Tietmeyer, a high-flying thinker who takes his
place in the great lineage of German idealist philosophy: 'It is
therefore necessary to restrain public spending and reduce
taxation to a level that is acceptable in the long term, to reform
the social welfare system, dismantle the rigidities in the labour
market, since a new phase of growth will only be attained if we
make an effort' – the 'we make' is magnificent – 'towards
flexibility in the labour market'. There you are: the big words
are out of the bag, and Mr Tietmeyer, in the great tradition of
German idealism, gives us a splendid example of the euphemis-
tic rhetoric which prevails in the money markets today.
Euphemism is essential in order to maintain the long-term
confidence of investors – which, it will have become clear, is the
alpha and omega of the whole economic system, the foundation
and ultimate goal, the *telos*, of the Europe of the future –
without provoking distrust or despair among the workers, who
in spite of everything also have to be taken into account if one
wants to have the new phase of growth the prospect of which
is dangled before them, in order to obtain the required effort
from them. For it is indeed from them that this effort is
expected, even if Mr Tietmeyer, who, it can be seen, is a past
master of the art of euphemism, does indeed say: 'dismantle the
rigidities in the labour market, since a new phase of growth will
only be attained if *we* make an effort towards flexibility in the
labour market.' This is splendid rhetorical work and may be
translated thus: 'Heave ho, workers! All together now, let's
make the effort of flexibility that *you* must provide!'

Instead of calmly proceeding to ask a question about the

external parity of the euro, its relations with the dollar and the yen, the *Le Monde* journalist, who is equally concerned not to discourage the investors, who read his paper and place large advertisements in it, might have asked Mr Tietmeyer what he understood by the key words in the language of the investors: 'rigidity in the labour market' and 'flexibility in the labour market'. The workers, if they were to read a paper as indisputably serious as *Le Monde*, would immediately understand what needs to be understood: night work, weekend work, irregular shifts, increased pressure, stress, etc. It can be seen that 'in the labour market' functions as a kind of Homeric epithet that can be attached to a certain number of words, and one might be tempted, in order to measure the flexibility of Mr Tietmeyer's language, to talk for example about flexibility or rigidity in the financial markets. The strangeness of this usage in Mr Tietmeyer's rigid discourse entitles us to suppose that there would be no question, in his mind, of "dismantling rigidities in the financial markets', or 'making an effort towards flexibility on the financial markets'. This leads us to think that, contrary to what is suggested by the 'we' in Mr Tietmeyer's 'if we make an effort', the workers alone are expected to make this effort and that they are the target of the threat, close to blackmail, contained in the sentence: 'since a new phase of growth will only be attained if we make an effort towards flexibility in the labour market'. To spell it out: Abandon *your* benefits today, so as not to destroy the confidence of the investors, for the sake of the growth that that will bring *us* tomorrow. This logic is well known to the workers concerned, who, to sum up the policy of 'participation' offered to them by Gaullism in times gone by, would say 'You give me your watch and I'll give you the time of day.'

After that commentary, I reread one last time the words of

Mr Tietmeyer: 'The crucial issue today is to create the conditions favourable to lasting growth, and the confidence of investors. It is therefore necessary...' – note the 'therefore' – 'to restrain public spending, reduce taxation to a level that is acceptable in the long term, to reform the welfare system, dismantle the rigidities in the labour market, since a new phase of growth will only be attained if we make an effort towards flexibility in the labour market.' If such an extraordinary text, so extraordinarily extraordinary, had every chance of passing unnoticed, living the brief life of the ephemeral writings in daily papers, this is because it was perfectly adjusted to the 'horizon of expectation' of the great majority of the readers of daily papers that we are. And that invites the question as to who produced and disseminated such a widespread 'horizon of expectation' (since the very least that needs to be added to reception theories, in which I am not a great believer, is the question of where that 'horizon' comes from). That horizon is the product of social, or rather political, work. If Mr Tietmeyer's words pass so readily, that is because they are common currency. They are everywhere, in every mouth, they circulate like legal tender, people accept them without hesitation, just as they would with currency, a stable, strong currency of course, as stable and worthy of confidence, belief, credit, as the deutschmark: 'lasting growth', 'investor confidence', 'public spending', 'welfare system', 'rigidity', 'labour market', 'flexibility', to which one should add 'globalization' (I learned from another newspaper I read in the aeroplane, showing how widespread the notion has become, that French chefs identify 'globalization' as a threat to the national cuisine . . .), 'deregulation', 'rate cuts' – without even saying which rates – 'competitiveness', 'productivity', etc.

This economic-sounding discourse would not be able to

circulate beyond the circle of its promoters without the collaboration of a host of people – politicians, journalists, and ordinary citizens with a tincture of economic culture sufficient to participate in the generalized circulation of the debased words of an economic vulgate. The questions of the journalist are one indication of the effect produced by media churning. He is so attuned to Mr Tietmeyer's expectations, so impregnated in advance with the answers, that he could have produced them himself. It is through such passive complicity that a view of the world that is called neo-liberal, but is in fact conservative, has progressively taken root, based on an atavistic faith in historical inevitability driven by the primacy of the productive forces unregulated except by the competing wills of the individual producers. And it is perhaps no accident that so many people of my generation have moved from a Marxist fatalism to a neo-liberal fatalism: in both cases, economism forbids responsibility and mobilization by cancelling out politics and imposing a whole set of unquestioned ends – maximum growth, competitiveness, productivity. To let oneself be guided by the President of the Bundesbank is to accept such a philosophy. What is surprising is that this fatalistic doctrine gives itself the air of a message of liberation, through a whole series of lexical tricks around the idea of freedom, liberation, deregulation, etc., a whole series of euphemisms or ambiguous uses of words – 'reform', for example – designed to present a restoration as a revolution, in a logic which is that of all conservative revolutions.

To conclude, let us come back to the key phrase in Mr Tietmeyer's discourse, the *confidence of the markets*. It has the virtue of bringing out clearly the historic choice which all those in power have to confront: between the confidence of the markets and the confidence of the people, they must choose. But the policy which aims to keep the confidence of the markets is likely to lose the confidence of the people. According to a recent survey of people's attitude to politicians, two-thirds of those questioned say that politicians are incapable of listening to and taking into account what the French population thinks. This complaint is particularly common among the supporters of the Front National – whose irresistible rise is deplored by political commentators who never think to make the connection between FN and IMF. (This despair at politicians is particularly marked in the age group 18 to 34, among manual and clerical workers and also among supporters of the Communist Party and the Front National. It is relatively high among the supporters of all parties, and rises to 64 per cent among supporters of the Socialist Party, a fact which is again not unconnected with the rise of the FN.) If the sacrosanct confidence of the markets is put in the context of the lack of confidence of the citizens, it perhaps becomes clearer where the root of the sickness is. Economics is, with a few exceptions, an abstract science based on the absolutely unjustifiable separation between the economic and the social which defines economism. This separation is the source of the failure of any policy that has no other end than to safeguard 'economic order and stability', the new Absolute of which Mr Tietmeyer has made himself the high priest, a failure to which the political blindness of some is leading us and of which we are all the victims.

Freiburg, October 1996

Social Scientists, Economic Science and the Social Movement

The social movement of December 1995 was a movement unprecedented in its scale and above all in its objectives. And if it was seen as extremely important by a large section of the French population and also by many people abroad, this is above all because it introduced some quite new objectives into social struggles. In a rough and confused form it outlined a genuine project for a society, collectively affirmed and capable of being put forward against what is being imposed by the dominant politics, by the revolutionary conservatives who are now in power, both in government and in the media.

Asking myself what social science researchers could offer to an undertaking like the États Généraux, I am convinced of the need for their presence in uncovering the specifically cultural and ideological dimension of this conservative revolution. The movement of last December received strong public support, because it was seen as a defence of the social advances, not of one particular category – even if one category was at the

Remarks at the inaugural meeting of the États Généraux du Mouvement Social, Paris, 23–4 Nov. 1996.

forefront, because it was particularly under attack – but of a
whole society, and even of a set of societies. These advances
concern work, public education, public transport, everything
which is public, and therefore the state, an institution which –
contrary to what some people would have us believe – is not
necessarily archaic and regressive.

It is no accident that this movement emerged in France; there
are historical reasons for that. But what ought to strike
observers is that it is continuing, being relayed, in France, in
various, unexpected ways – the truck drivers' action: who would
have expected it in that form? – and also in Europe: in Spain,
right now; in Greece, a few years ago; in Germany, where the
movement took inspiration from the French movement and has
explicitly declared its affinities with it; in Korea – which is even
more important, for symbolic and practical reasons. This kind
of rotating struggle is, it seems to me, searching for its
theoretical unity and above all its practical unity. The French
movement can be seen as the vanguard of a worldwide struggle
against neo-liberalism and against the new conservative revolution, in which the symbolic dimension is extremely important.
One of the weaknesses of all progressive movements lies in the
fact that they have underestimated the importance of this
dimension and have not always forged appropriate weapons to
fight on this front. Social movements are several symbolic
revolutions behind their opponents, who use media consultants,
public relations consultants and so on.

The conservative revolution calls itself neo-liberal, thereby
giving itself a scientific air, and the capacity to act as a theory.
One of the theoretical and practical errors of many theories –
starting with the Marxist theory – has been the failure to take
account of the power of theory. We must no longer make that
mistake. We are dealing with opponents who are armed with

theories, and I think they need to be fought with intellectual and cultural weapons. In pursuing that struggle, because of the division of labour some are better armed than others, because it is their job. And some of them are ready to set to work. What can they offer? First of all, a certain authority. What name was given to the people who supported the government last December? Experts, although the whole lot of them together did not have the beginnings of the making of an economist. That authority effect has to be fought with an authority effect.

But that is not all. The force of social authority, which is exerted on the social movement and right into the depths of the workers' minds, is very great. It produces a form of demoralization. And one of the reasons for its strength is that it is held by people who all seem to agree with one another – consensus is in general a sign of truth. Another is that it is based on the apparently most powerful instruments now available to thought, in particular mathematics. The role of what is called the dominant ideology is fulfilled nowadays by a certain use of mathematics (I exaggerate, but it is a way of drawing attention to the fact that the work of rationalization – giving reasons to justify things that are often unjustifiable – has now found a very powerful instrument in mathematical economics). This ideology, which dresses up simply conservative thought in the guise of pure reason, has to be fought, with reasons, arguments, refutations, demonstrations; and this implies scientific work.

One of the strengths of neo-liberal thought is that it presents itself as a kind of 'great chain of Being', as in the old theological metaphor, where at one end there is God and then you work your way down, link by link, to the lowest forms of life. In the neo-liberal universe, right at the top, in the place of God, is a mathematician, and at the bottom there is an ideologue of *Esprit*,[1] who doesn't know much about economics but wants to give the impression of knowing something, with the aid of a varnish of technical vocabulary. This very powerful chain has an authority effect. There are doubts, even among activists, which partly result from the essentially social strength of the theory which gives authority to the words of Mr Trichet or Mr Tietmeyer, the President of the Bundesbank, or this or that essayist. It is not a sequence of demonstrations, it is a chain of authorities which runs from the mathematician to the banker, from the banker to the philosopher-journalist, from the essayist to the journalist. It is also a channel for the circulation of money and all sorts of economic and social advantages, international invitations, consideration. We sociologists, without denouncing anyone, can undertake to map out these networks and show how the circulation of ideas is subtended by a circulation of power. There are people who exchange ideological services for positions of power. Examples would be needed, but it is sufficient to read the list of signatories of the famous 'Petition of experts'. What is interesting is that the hidden connections between people who normally work in isolation – even if we often see them appearing in pairs in false debates on television — and between foundations, associations, journals, etc., are then revealed to the light of day.

Collectively, in the mode of consensus, these people utter a fatalistic discourse which consists of transforming economic tendencies into destiny. Now, social laws, economic laws and so on only take effect to the extent that people let them do so. And if conservatives favour laissez-faire, this is because in general these tendential laws conserve, and they need laissez-faire in order to conserve. Those of the financial markets, in particular, which are we endlessly told about, are laws of conservation, which need laissez-faire in order to operate.

One would need to develop this, argue it, and above all

nuance it. I apologize for the somewhat simplifying character of what I have said. As for the social movement, it can be satisfied with existing: it annoys enough people just like that, and no one is going to ask it in addition to produce justifications – whereas intellectuals who associate themselves with the social movement are immediately asked: 'But what are you proposing?' We shouldn't fall into the trap of offering a programme. There are quite enough parties and apparatuses for that. What we can do is to create, not a counter-programme, but a structure for collective research, interdisciplinary and international, bringing together social scientists, activists, representatives of activists, etc., with the social scientists being placed in a quite definite role: they can participate in a particularly effective way, because it's their job, in working parties and seminars, in association with people who are in the movement.

This rules out from the start a certain number of roles: social scientists are not fellow-travellers, in other words hostages and guarantors, figureheads and alibis who sign petitions and who are disposed of as soon as they have been used; nor are they Zhdanovian apparatchiks who come in to exercise apparently intellectual powers within the social movements which they cannot exercise in intellectual life; nor are they experts coming in to give lessons – not even anti-expert experts; nor are they prophets who will provide answers to all questions about the social movement and its future. They are people who can help to define the function of meetings like this one. Or who can point out that the people here are not present as spokespersons, but as citizens who come into a place of discussion and research, with ideas, with arguments, leaving their slogans, platforms and party habits in the cloakroom. This is not always easy. Among the party habits which threaten to come back are the creation of committees, composite motions often prepared in advance, and so on. Sociology teaches how groups function and how to make use of the laws governing the way they function so as to try to circumvent them.

There is a need to invent new forms of communication between researchers and activists, which means a new division of labour between them. One of the missions which sociologists can fulfil perhaps better than anyone is the fight against saturation by the media. We all hear ready-made phrases all day long. You can't turn on the radio without hearing about the 'global village', 'globalization', and so on. These are innocent-sounding words, but through them come a whole philosophy and a whole worldview which engender fatalism and submission. We can block this forced feeding by criticizing the words, by helping non-professionals to equip themselves with specific weapons of resistance, so as to combat the effects of authority and the grip of television, which plays an absolutely crucial role. It is no longer possible nowadays to conduct social struggles without having a specific programme for fighting with and against television. I commend to you Patrick Champagne's book, *Faire l'opinion*, which ought to be a kind of manual for the political campaigner. In that battle, the fight against the media intellectuals is important. Personally, those people do not cause me sleepless nights, and I never think about them when I write, but they have an extremely important role from a political standpoint, and it would be desirable for a proportion of the researchers to agree to devote some of their time and energy, in their activist mode, to countering their effects.

A further objective has to be to invent new forms of symbolic action. On this point, I think that social movements, with a few historic exceptions, have a lot of ground to make up. In his book, Patrick Champagne shows how some big mobilizations may receive less coverage in the newspapers and on television than some minuscule demonstrations that are put on in a way that interests the journalists. It is clearly not a question of fighting against the journalists, who are themselves subject to the constraints of job insecurity, with all the effects of censorship it produces in all the professions of cultural production. But it is essential to realize that an enormous part of what we may say or do will be filtered, in other words often annihilated, by what the journalists will say about it. Including what we are about to do here. And that is a remark that they won't reproduce in their reporting.

To conclude, I will say that one of the problems is to be reflexive – a grand word, but it is not used gratuitously. Our objective is not only to invent responses, but to invent a way of inventing responses, to invent a new form of organization of the work of contestation and of organization of contestation, of the task of activism. Our dream, as social scientists, might be for part of our research to be useful to the social movement, instead of being lost, as is often the case nowadays, because it is intercepted and distorted by journalists or by hostile interpreters, etc. In the framework of groups like Raisons d'Agir, we would like to invent new forms of expression that make it possible to communicate the most advanced findings of research. But that also presupposes a change of language and outlook on the part of the researchers.

To return to the social movement, I think, as I said a moment ago, that we are witnessing successive waves – I could also have mentioned the students' and teachers' strikes in Belgium, the strikes in Italy, etc. – of struggle against neo-liberal imperialism, struggles which generally do not recognize each other (and which may take forms which are not always appealing, like some forms of fundamentalism). So at the very least there is a need to unify international information and enable it to

circulate. There is a need to reinvent internationalism, which
was hijacked by Soviet imperialism, in other words to invent
forms of theoretical thought and forms of practical action
capable of operating at the level where the fight has to take
place. If it is true that most of the dominant economic forces
operate at world level, transnationally, it is also true that there
is an empty space, that of transnational struggles. It is
theoretically empty, because it has not been thought through,
and it is practically empty, for lack of genuine international
organization of the forces capable of countering the new
conservative revolution, at least on a European scale.

Paris, November 1996

Notes

1 Intellectual journal associated with 'Christian personalist'
  thinking and the focus of intellectual support for the Juppé
  reforms (trans.).

For a New Internationalism

The peoples of Europe are now at a turning-point in their history, because the conquests of several centuries of social struggles, of intellectual and political battles for the dignity of workers, are directly threatened. The movements that are seen, first in one place, then in another, throughout Europe, and elsewhere, even in Korea, these movements that follow on from one another, in Germany, France, Greece, Italy, etc., apparently without real coordination, are so many revolts against a policy which takes different forms in different fields and in different countries but which, nevertheless, is always inspired by the same intention, that of removing the social entitlements which are, whatever people say, among the highest achievements of civilization – achievements that ought to be universalized, extended to the whole planet, globalized, instead of using the pretext of 'globalization', of the competition from economically and socially less advanced countries, in order to cast doubt on them. Nothing is more natural or more legitimate

Remarks at the third international forum of the Deutscher Gewerkschaftsbund (DGB) of Hesse, Frankfurt, 7 June 1997.

than the defence of these entitlements, which some people want
to present as a form of conservatism or archaism. Would anyone
condemn as conservative the defence of the cultural achievements of humanity, Kant or Hegel, Mozart or Beethoven? The
social entitlements that I am referring to, the right to work, a
health and welfare system, for which men and women have
suffered and fought, are achievements which are just as
important and precious, and, moreover, they do not only
survive in museums, libraries and academies, but are living and
active in people's lives and govern their everyday existence.
That is why I cannot help feeling something like a sense of
scandal at those who make themselves the allies of the most
brutal economic forces and who condemn the people who, in
fighting to defend their entitlements, sometimes described as
'privileges', defend the rights of all the men and women of
Europe and elsewhere.

The challenge I made a few months ago to Mr Tietmeyer has
often been misunderstood. It was often taken as an answer to
a question which is wrongly posed, precisely because it is posed
in terms of the logic of the neo-liberal thinking to which Mr
Tietmeyer subscribes. According to that view, monetary integration, symbolized by the creation of the euro, is the obligatory
preliminary, the necessary and sufficient condition, for the
political integration of Europe. In other words it is assumed that
the political integration of Europe will flow necessarily, ineluc-
tably, from economic integration. It follows that anyone who
opposes the policy of monetary integration, and opposes its
advocates, like Mr Tietmeyer, will be taken to oppose political
integration, in a word, to be 'against Europe'.

Not at all. What is in question is the role of the state (the
currently existing national states, or the European state to be
created), particularly as regards the protection of social rights,

the role of the social state, which alone can stand up to the
implacable mechanisms of the economy relinquished to itself.
One can be against a Europe which, like that of Mr Tietmeyer,
would serve as a relay for the financial markets, while being for
a Europe which, through a concerted policy, blocks the way of
the uncontrolled violence of those markets. But there is no
reason to hope for such a policy from the bankers' Europe that
is being prepared for us. Monetary integration cannot be
expected to secure social integration. On the contrary: for we
know that countries that want to maintain their competitiveness within the euro zone relative to their partners will have no
option but to reduce wage costs by reducing welfare contributions. 'Social dumping' and wage-cutting, the 'flexibilization' of
the labour market, will be the only devices left to states which
can no longer play on exchange rates. Added to these mechanisms will undoubtedly be the pressure of the 'monetary
authorities', like the Bundesbank and its leaders, who are
always eager to preach 'wage restraint'. Only a European social
state would be capable of countering the *disintegratory* effects
of monetary economics. But Mr Tietmeyer and the neo-liberals
do not want either national states, which they see as simple
obstacles to the free functioning of the economy, or, *a fortiori*,
the supranational state, which they want to reduce to a bank.
And it is clear that, if they want to get rid of the national states
(or the Council of Ministers of Community states) by stripping
them of their power, this is not in order to create a supranational
state which, with enhanced authority, would impose on them
the constraints, especially as regards social policy, from which
they want at all costs to be freed.

So it is possible to be hostile to the integration of Europe
based solely on the single currency, without being in any way
hostile to the political integration of Europe; and while calling,

on the contrary, for the creation of a European state capable of controlling the European Bank and, more precisely, capable of controlling, by anticipating, the social effects of a union reduced to its purely monetary dimension, in accordance with the neoliberal philosophy which aims to sweep away all the vestiges of the (social) state as so many obstacles to the harmonious functioning of the markets.

It is certain that international (and more especially intra-European) competition is an obstacle to the application *in one country* of what you call the 'ban on social regression'. That is seen clearly as regards the reduction of the working week or reflation of the economy (despite the fact that a reduced working week is partly self-financing because of the likely increase in productivity and that it is offset by a reduction of the huge amounts spent on unemployment). The British Prime Minister John Major understood this perfectly well when he said cynically: 'You will have the wage costs and we will have the jobs.' It has also been understood by the German employers who are starting to relocate some of their production in France, where the destruction of social rights is relatively more 'advanced'. In fact, however, if it is true that competition is for the most part intra-European and that it is French workers taking jobs away from German workers, and vice versa – as is indeed the case, since *almost three-quarters of the external trade of European countries takes place within the confines of Europe* – it can be seen that the effects of a reduced working week without loss of wages would be very limited if such a measure were decided and applied on a European scale.

The same is true of policies for the revival of demand or for investment in the new technologies: though they may be impossible or ruinous, as the orthodoxy has it, so long as they are carried out in a single country, they become reasonable on the scale of a continent. It is also true, more generally, of any action oriented by the principles of an economics of happiness, which would take account of all the profits and all the costs, material and symbolic, of human behaviours and in particular of activity or inactivity. In short, in place of the monetary Europe that is destroying social gains it is urgent that we put forward a social Europe based on an alliance between the workers of the various European countries, one that is capable of neutralizing attempts to use the workers of each country against the workers of all the others, in particular through 'social dumping'.

To achieve this, and to move beyond a mere abstract programme, it would be necessary to invent a new internationalism, a task which falls, first and foremost, to the trade union organizations. But internationalism, as well as having been discredited, in its traditional form, by its subordination to Soviet imperialism, comes up against great obstacles due to the fact that union structures are national ones (linked to the state and in part produced by the state), separated by different historical traditions. For example, in Germany, there is a strong autonomy of the 'social partners', whereas in France there is a tradition of weak trade unions facing a strong state. Equally, the welfare system takes very different forms, from Britain where it is financed by taxation to Germany and France where it is paid for by contributions. At the European level, there is almost nothing. What is called 'social Europe', which is of little interest to the 'guardians of the euro', amounts to a few grand principles, with for example the Community Charter of Fundamental Social Rights defining a set of minimum standards, with implementation being left to the discretion of member states. The social protocol annexed to the Maastricht treaty provides for the adoption by qualified majority of directives in the areas of working conditions, information to and consultation of workers, and equal treatment of men and women. It also gave the European 'social partners' the option to negotiate collective agreements which, when adopted by the Council of Ministers, have the force of law.

All that is well and good, but where is the European social force capable of imposing such agreements on the European employers? The international structures, such as the European Trade Union Confederation, are weak (for example, they exclude a number of unions such as the CGT) in the face of organized employers, and, paradoxically, they almost always leave the initiative to the Community institutions (and the technocrats), even when social rights are at stake. The European works councils could be a powerful recourse, as has been seen in some conflicts within multinational corporations, but they are only consultative bodies and are hindered by the differences of interest which divide them within, or which set them against each other between one country and another. The European coordination of workers' struggles has a lot of ground to make up. The trade union organizations have missed some major opportunities, such as the strike in Germany for the 35-hour week, which was not taken up at the European level, or the great mobilizations which occurred in France in late 1995 and early 1996, against the austerity policy and the dismantling of the public services. The intellectuals – especially in Germany – have remained silent, when they have not simply echoed the dominant discourse.

How are the foundations to be laid for a new internationalism among the trade unions, the intellectuals and the peoples of Europe? There are two possible forms of action, and they are not mutually exclusive. One is the mobilization of the peoples, which presupposes, in this case, a specific contribution by the intellectuals in as much as demobilization partly results from the demoralization produced by the permanent action of 'propaganda' by essayists and journalists, a propaganda which neither the authors nor the recipients perceive as such. The social bases for the success of such a mobilization exist: I will only mention the effects of the transformations of the educational system, with, in particular, the rising levels of education, the devaluation of qualifications and the resulting structural deskilling, and also the blurring of the separation between students and manual workers (there is still a separation between the old and the young, between those in secure jobs and those facing job insecurity or proletarianization, but real connections have been made, through, for example, educated manual workers' children affected by the crisis). But also, and above all, there is the evolution of the social structure, with – contrary to the myth of the enormous middle class, which is so widespread in Germany – the growth in social inequality, the overall income from capital having risen by 60 per cent while the income from waged labour has remained stable. This action of international mobilization presupposes that an important role is given to the battle of ideas (breaking with the *ouvriériste* tradition which pervades social movements, especially in France, and which refuses to give intellectual struggles their rightful place in social struggles), and in particular to critique of the representations continuously produced and propagated by the dominant groups and their lackeys in the media: false statistics, myths about full employment in Britain or the US, and so on.

The second form of intervention in favour of an internationalism capable of promoting a transnational social state is action on and through the national states, which, at the present time, for lack of an overall vision of the future, are incapable of managing the general interest of the Community. We have to act on the national states, firstly to defend and strengthen the historical advances associated with the national states (which are greatest and most rooted in people's minds where the state has been strongest, as in France); and secondly to force these states to work for the creation of a European social state combining the greatest social advances of the various national states (more nurseries, schools and hospitals, fewer soldiers, policemen and prisons) and to subordinate the creation of the single market to the implementation of the social measures designed to counter the likely social consequences that un-bridled competition will have for wage-earners. (We might take example here from Sweden which has rejected entry into the euro until there is a renegotiation giving priority to the coordination of economic and social policies.) Social cohesion is as important a goal as stable exchange rates and social harmonization is the precondition for the success of a genuine monetary union.

If social harmonization, and the solidarity that it produces and presupposes, are made an absolute precondition, then a number of common objectives must be negotiated immediately, with the same concern for rigour hitherto reserved for economic indicators (such as the sacrosanct 3 per cent in the Maastricht Treaty): these include the definition of *minimum wages* (differentiated by zones to take account of regional disparities); bringing in measures *against the corruption and tax fraud* which reduce the contribution of financial activities to public spending, indirectly resulting in excessive taxation of labour, and *against social dumping* between directly competing activities; drawing up a code of *common social rights* which, while accepting a transitional differentiation between zones, would aim to integrate social policies by merging them where they exist and developing them where they do not exist, with for example the

definition of a minimum income for persons without paid
employment and without other resources, reduction of employees' contributions, development of social rights such as training,
the definition of the right to employment and housing and the
invention of an external policy in social matters aimed at
spreading and generalizing European social standards; a *common investment policy* corresponding to the general interest – in
contrast to the investment strategies resulting from the
autonomization of financial activities that are purely speculative and/or directed towards short-term profit, or based on
assumptions totally contrary to the general interest, such as the
belief that reductions in employment are an index of good
management and a guarantee of efficiency, priority would be
given to strategies aimed at safeguarding non-renewable resources and the environment, developing trans-European transport and energy networks, developing public housing and urban
regeneration (especially through non-polluting urban transport), investment in research and development in health and the
protection of the environment, the financing of new and
apparently more risky activities, in forms unknown to the
financial world (small businesses, self-employment).[1]

What may look like a simple catalogue of disparate measures
is in fact inspired by the will to break out of the fatalism of neo-
liberal thinking, to 'defatalize' by politicizing, by replacing the
naturalized economy of neo-liberalism with an economy of
happiness, based on human initiatives and will, making allow-
ance in its calculations for the costs in suffering and the profits
in fulfilment that are ignored by the strictly economistic cult of
productivity and profitability.

The future of Europe depends a great deal on the strength of
the progressive forces in Germany (trade unions, SPD, Greens)
and on their will and capacity to resist the 'strong euro' policy

advocated by the Bundesbank and the German government. It will also depend on their capacity to stimulate and relay the movement for a reorientation of European policy which is already making itself heard in several countries, in particular in France. In short, against all the prophets of misery who want to convince you that your destiny is in the hands of transcendent, independent, indifferent powers, such as 'the financial markets' or the mechanisms of 'globalization', I want to declare, with the hope of convincing you, that the future, your future, which is also our future, that of all Europeans, depends a great deal on you, as Germans and as trade unionists.

Frankfurt, June 1997

Notes

1 I borrow a number of these suggestions from Yves Salesse, *Propositions pour une autre Europe: construire Babel.*

Return to Television

Q In your book On Television, *you say that it is necessary to awaken the consciousness of media professionals to the invisible structures of broadcasting. Do you think that the professionals and the public are really still so blind to the mechanisms of the media in a world in which the media are so present? Or is there complicity between them?*

PB I don't think the professionals are blind. I think they live in a state of dual consciousness: a practical view which leads them to get as much as they can, sometimes cynically, sometimes without realizing it, out of the possibilities offered by the media tool at their disposal (I am talking about the most *powerful* of them); and a theoretical view, moralizing and full of indulgence towards themselves, which leads them to deny publicly what they do, to mask it and even mask it from themselves. Two items of evidence: the reactions to my little book, which the 'leading commentators' unanimously and

Interview with P. R. Pires, in *O Globo* (Rio de Janeiro), 4 Oct. 1997, after the publication of the Portugese translation of *On Television*.

violently condemned as outrageous while proclaiming each more
insistently than the other that it contained nothing that was not
already known (a truly Freudian logic which I also saw in the
reactions to my books on education); and the pontificating,
hypocritical commentaries they produced on the role of the
journalists in the death of Princess Diana while themselves
allowing the journalistic possibilities of this non-event to be
exploited beyond the bounds of decency. This split consciousness
– very common among the powerful ... it was said that the
Roman augurs could not look at each other without laughing –
means that they can both condemn the objective description of
their practice as a scandalous denunciation or a poisonous
pamphlet, and say equivalent things out loud when speaking
privately or even for the benefit of the sociologist who interviews
them (I give examples of this in my book) or indeed even in
public statements. Thus Thomas Ferenczi writes in *Le Monde* of
7–8 September, in response to readers' complaints about the
paper's treatment of the Princess Diana story, that, yes, '*Le
Monde* has changed' and is devoting more and more space to
what he discreetly calls 'faits de société' – just the truths which
he could not bear to see uttered only three months earlier. At
a time when the slippage, *imposed by television*, is there for all
to see, the paper flaunts it, in the appropriately moralizing tone,
as a way of adapting to modernity and 'enlarging its curiosity'!
(*Added in January 1998*: And the 'Ombudsman' [*médiateur*]
specially mandated to fob off readers conscious of the ever-
growing weight of commercial preoccupations in editorial
choices now deploys all his rhetoric to try to prove that one can
be the judge in one's own case, while endlessly rehearsing the
same tautological arguments. To those who, after the publication of an interview with a fading pop star by an insipid writer,[1]
complain that *Le Monde* is 'drifting into a kind of demagogy',

he can only reply, in the edition dated 18–19 January 1998, that his paper is 'committed to openness': 'These subjects, and others,' he writes, 'receive extensive coverage because they shed useful light on the world around us and because, for that very reason, they interest a large section of our readership.' To those who, the previous week, condemned the indulgent report by a journalist-intellectual on the situation in Algeria, a betrayal of all the critical ideals of the tradition of the intellectual, he replies, in *Le Monde* dated 25–6 January 1998, that it is not for the journalist to choose between intellectuals. The texts thus produced, week after week, by the defender of the line of the newspaper, no doubt chosen for his extreme prudence, are the greatest imprudence of the paper: the deep unconscious of journalism is progressively revealed, as the readers make their challenges, in a kind of long weekly session of psychoanalysis.) So, split consciousness among the dominant professionals, the nomenklatura of star journalists bound together by common interests and complicities of all kinds.[2] Among 'rank-and-file' journalists, the pieceworkers of journalism, the freelancers, all those who earn a precarious living by doing what is most authentically journalistic in journalism, there is, naturally, more lucidity and it is often expressed very directly. It's in part thanks to their testimony that it is possible to learn something about what goes on in the world of television.[3]

Q   You analyse the formation of what you call the 'journalistic field', but your point of view is that of the 'sociological field'. Do you think there is an incompatibility between those two fields? Does sociology present 'truths' and the media present 'lies'?

PB   You are introducing a dichotomy very characteristic of the journalistic vision, which – it's one of its most typical

properties – is inclined to be Manichean. It goes without saying
that journalists produce some truth and sociologists produce
some untruth. In a field, you find everything, by definition! But
perhaps in different proportions and with different probabili-
ties ... Having said that, the first task of the sociologist is to
explode that way of formulating questions. And I say in my
little book, several times, that sociologists can help lucid and
critical journalists (there are a lot of them, but not necessarily
in the top jobs in television, radio and the press) by providing
them with instruments of knowledge and understanding, perhaps sometimes of action, that would enable them to work with
some effectiveness towards withstanding the economic and
social forces that bear on them, particularly by allying with
social science researchers, whom they often see as enemies. I'm
currently trying (in particular through the magazine *Liber*) to
create those kinds of international connections between journalists and researchers and to develop forces of *resistance* against
the forces of oppression which weigh on journalism and which
journalism brings to bear upon the whole of cultural production
and, through that, the whole of society.

*Q Television is identified as a form of symbolic oppression. What
is the democratic potential of television and the media?*

PB There is an enormous gap between the image that media
people have and give of the media and the reality of their action
and influence. The media are, overall, a factor of depoliticization,
which naturally acts more strongly on the most depoliticized
sections of the public, on women more than men, on the less
educated more than the more educated, on the poor more than
the rich. It may be a scandalous thing to say this, but it is clearly
established from statistical analysis of the probability of

formulating an explicit response to a political question or of abstaining (the consequences of this fact, especially in politics, are explored at some length in my recent book *Méditations pascaliennes*). Television (much more than the newspapers) offers an increasingly depoliticized, aseptic, bland view of the world, and it is increasingly dragging down the newspapers in its slide into demagogy and subordination to commercial values. The Princess Diana affair is a perfect example of everything I say in my book, a sort of paroxysm. It is all there at once: a 'human interest' story that entertains; the telethon effect, by which I mean the uncontroversial defence of humanitarian causes that are vague, ecumenical and above all perfectly apolitical. You get the sense that with that event, coming just after the Pope's youth rally in Paris and just before the death of Mother Teresa, the last restraints gave way. (Mother Teresa, who so far as I know was no progressive in relation to abortion and women's liberation, fitted perfectly into this world governed by hard-nosed bankers, who have nothing against pious defenders of humanity who come and bandage the wounds which they see as inevitable and which they have helped to inflict.) And so we saw *Le Monde, two weeks after the accident*, devoting its main front-page story to the progress of the inquiry into the crash, while on the TV news the massacres in Algeria and relations between Israel and Palestine were relegated to a few minutes at the end of the programme. Incidentally, you were saying a moment ago, lies from journalists, truth from sociologists: I can tell you, as a sociologist who knows Algeria fairly well, that I have great admiration for the newspaper *La Croix*, which has recently published a very precise, rigorous and courageous dossier on what is really behind the massacres there. The question I ask myself – and so far the answer is negative – is whether the other newspapers, and in particular those which

make high claims for their seriousness, will pursue those
analyses . . .

*Q   In terms of the famous dichotomy put forward by Umberto Eco
in the 1960s, could we say that you are 'apocalyptic' as opposed to
'integrated'?*

PB   It's a way of putting it. There are certainly a lot of
'integrated' people about. And the strength of the new dominant order is that it has found the specific means of 'integrating'
(in some cases you might say buying, in others seducing) an
ever-growing fraction of the intellectuals, all over the world.
These 'integrated' intellectuals often continue to see themselves
as critical (or simply on the left), according to the traditional
model. And that helps to give great symbolic efficacy to their
work in rallying support for the established order.

*Q   What is your opinion on the role of the media in the Diana
affair?*

PB   It's a perfect, almost uncannily extreme illustration of
what I was describing in my book. The royal families of Monaco,
England and elsewhere will be kept on as inexhaustible
reservoirs of plots for soap operas and *telenovelas*. In any case
it is clear that the great media 'happening' provoked by the
death of Princess Diana fits perfectly into the series of
entertainments which enthral the petite bourgeoisie of England
and other countries, along with musicals like *Evita* or *Jesus
Christ Superstar*, born of the marriage of melodrama and high-
tech special effects, mawkish TV serials, sentimental films,
airport novels, 'music for easy listening', 'family entertainments', and all those other products of the cultural industry,

poured out all day long by conformist and cynical television and radio channels and combining the lachrymose moralism of the churches with the aesthetic conservatism of bourgeois entertainments.

Q   What is the possible role of the intellectuals in the 'mediated' world?

PB   It is not certain that they can play the great positive role of the inspired prophet that they sometimes tend to take upon themselves in periods of euphoria. It would be at least something if they could refrain from entering into complicity and collaboration with the forces which threaten to destroy the very bases of their existence and their freedom, in other words the forces of the market. It took several centuries, as I showed in my book *The Rules of Art*, for jurists, artists, writers and scientists to gain their autonomy with respect to the political, religious and economic powers, and to be able to impose their own norms, their specific values, in particular of truth, in their own universe, their microcosm, and sometimes in the social world (Zola in the Dreyfus affair, Sartre and the 121 in the Algerian war, etc.). These conquests of freedom are sometimes threatened, and not only by colonels, dictators and mafias. They are threatened by more insidious forces, those of the market, but transfigured, reincarnated in models that seduce one group or another: for some, it is the figure of the economist armed with mathematical formalism, who describes the evolution of the 'globalized' economy as a destiny; for others, the figure of the international star of rock, pop or rap, presenting a lifestyle that is both chic and facile (for the first time in history, the seductions of snobbery have become attached to practices and products typical of mass consumption, such as denim, T-shirts and Coca-Cola); for others a 'campus radicalism' labelled postmodern and offering the seductive glamour of seemingly revolutionary celebration of cultural pick-and-mix, and so on. If there is one area where the 'globalization' that is on the lips of all 'integrated' intellectuals is a reality, it is precisely that of cultural mass production – television (I'm thinking in particular of the *telenovelas* that have become a Latin American speciality and which propagate a 'Diana' view of the world), popular cinema and magazines, or even, which is much more serious, 'social thinking' for the 'quality press', with themes and words that circle the planet, like 'the end of history', 'postmodernism', or . . . 'globalization'. Artists, writers and researchers (especially sociologists) have the capacity, and the duty, to combat the most malign of the threats that this global production implies for culture and democracy.

Notes

1 Johnny Halliday, interviewed by Daniel Rondeau (trans.).
2 On these complicities, see Halimi, *Les Nouveaux Chiens de garde*.
3 See for example the excellent analyses presented in Accardo et al., *Journalistes au quotidien: outils pour une socioanalyse des pratiques journalistiques*.

The Government Finds the People Irresponsible

We have had enough of the slipperiness and prevarication of all the politicians, elected by us, who declare us 'irresponsible' when we remind them of the promises they made us. We have had enough of the state racism which they authorize. This very day, a friend of mine, a French citizen of Algerian origin, told me what happened to his daughter when she went to re-enrol at the university: at the mere sight of her Arab-looking name, the university employee asked her, as if it were the most natural thing in the world, to show her papers and her passport. To put an end once and for all to all these bullyings and humiliations, which would have been unthinkable a few years ago, we need to make a clear break with hypocritical legislation which is no more than an immense concession to the xenophobia of the Front National. This naturally means repealing the Pasqua and Debré laws, but above all it means putting an end to all the hypocritical language of all the politicians who, at a time when

Text published in *Les Inrockuptibles*, 8 Oct. 1997, on the bills of ministers Guigou (Justice) and Chevènement (Interior) on French nationality and the residence of foreigners in France.

the country is being reminded of the implication of the French authorities in the extermination of the Jews, practically give a free hand to all those in the administration who are in a position to express their most stupidly xenophobic impulses, like the university employee I mentioned a moment ago. There is no point in engaging in subtle legal discussions about the merits of this or that law. What we must do is simply repeal a law which, by its very existence, legitimates the discriminatory practices of civil servants, at every level, by helping to cast a generalized suspicion on foreigners – and not just *any* foreigners, of course. What does it mean to be a citizen if at any moment proof of citizenship has to be produced? (Many French parents of Algerian origin wonder what first names they should give their children to spare them problems later. And the employee who harassed my friend's daughter expressed surprise that she was called Mélanie . . .)

I say that a law is racist when it authorizes any civil servant to cast doubt on the citizenship of a citizen at the mere sight of her face or the sound of her name, as happens now, thousands of times every day. It is regrettable that in the highly controlled government which has been offered to us by Mr Jospin, there is not a single bearer of one of the stigmata subject to the irreproachable arbitrariness of the functionaries of the French state, a black face or an Arabic-sounding name, to remind Mr Chevènement that there is a difference between law and behaviour and that there are laws which authorize the worst behaviour. I offer all this for consideration by all those who are now silent and indifferent and who will come back in thirty years to express their 'repentance',[1] at a time when young French citizens of Algerian origin will have the first name Kelkal.[2]

Paris, October 1997

Notes

1 The French bishops have collectively expressed their 'repent-ance' over the attitude of the French hierarchy during the German occupation (trans.).
2 Kelkal is the name of a young Algerian, a member of a terrorist network, who was shot by the police (trans.).

Job Insecurity is Everywhere Now

The collective thinking that has gone on here in the last two days is an entirely original undertaking, because it has brought together people who have little opportunity to meet and exchange their views – civil servants and politicians, trade unionists, economists and sociologists, people in jobs, often insecure ones, and people without jobs. I would like to comment on some of the problems which have been discussed. The first one, which is tacitly excluded from academic meetings, is: what is the final outcome of these debates, or, more brutally, what is the point of all these intellectual discussions? Paradoxically, it is the academics who most worry about this question or whom this question most worries (I am thinking in particular of the economists here present, who are rather unrepresentative of a profession in which very few are concerned with social reality or indeed with reality at all) who have had it put most directly to them (and it is undoubtedly a good thing that this should be so). Both brutal and naive, it reminds the academics of their

Intervention at the Rencontres Européennes contre la Précarité, Grenoble, 12–13 Dec. 1997.

responsibilities, which may be very great, at least when, by their
silence or their complicity, they contribute to the maintenance
of the symbolic order which is the condition of the functioning
of the economic order.

It has emerged clearly that job insecurity is now everywhere:
in the private sector, but also in the public sector, which has
greatly increased the number of temporary, part-time or casual
positions; in industry, but also in the institutions of cultural
production and diffusion – education, journalism, the media,
etc. In all these areas it produces more or less identical effects,
which become particularly visible in the extreme case of the
unemployed: the destructuring of existence, which is deprived
among other things of its temporal structures, and the ensuing
deterioration of the whole relationship to the world, time and
space. Casualization profoundly affects the person who suffers
it: by making the whole future uncertain, it prevents all rational
anticipation and, in particular, the basic belief and hope in the
future that one needs in order to rebel, especially collectively,
against present conditions, even the most intolerable.

Added to these effects of precariousness on those directly
touched by it there are the effects on all the others, who are
apparently spared. The awareness of it never goes away: it is
present at every moment in everyone's mind (except, no doubt,
in the minds of the liberal economists, perhaps because, as one
of their theoretical opponents has pointed out, they enjoy the
protection afforded by tenured positions . . .). It pervades both
the conscious and the unconscious mind. The existence of a large
reserve army, which, because of the overproduction of graduates, is no longer restricted to the lowest levels of competence
and technical qualification, helps to give all those in work the
sense that they are in no way irreplaceable and that their work,
their jobs, are in some way a privilege, a fragile, threatened

privilege (as they are reminded by their employers as soon as
they step out of line and by journalists and commentators at the
first sign of a strike). Objective insecurity gives rise to a
generalized subjective insecurity which is now affecting all
workers in our highly developed economy. This kind of
'collective mentality' (I use this expression, although I do not
much like it, to make myself understood), common to the whole
epoch, is the origin of the demoralization and loss of militancy
which one can observe (as I did in Algeria in the 1960s) in
underdeveloped countries suffering very high rates of unemployment or underemployment and permanently haunted by
the spectre of joblessness.

The unemployed and the casualized workers, having suffered
a blow to their capacity to project themselves into the future,
which is the precondition for all so-called rational conducts,
starting with economic calculation, or, in a quite different
realm, political organization, are scarcely capable of being
mobilized. Paradoxically, as I showed in *Travail et travailleurs
en Algérie*,[1] my oldest and perhaps most contemporary book, in
order to conceive a revolutionary project, in other words a
reasoned ambition to transform the present by reference to a
projected future, one needs some grasp on the present. The
proletarian, unlike the subproletarian, does have this basic
minimum of present assurances, security, which is needed in
order to conceive the ambition of changing the present with an
eye to the future. But, let me say in passing, the worker is also
someone who has something to defend, something to lose, a job,
even if it is exhausting and badly paid, and a number of the
things the worker does, sometimes described as too prudent or
even conservative, spring from the fear of falling lower, back
into the subproletariat.

When unemployment rises to very high levels, as it has in a

number of European countries, and when job insecurity affects a very high proportion of the population – manual workers, clerical workers in commerce and industry, but also journalists, teachers and students, work becomes a rare commodity, desirable at any price, which puts employees at the mercy of employers, who exploit and abuse the power this gives them. Competition for work tends to generate a struggle of all against all, which destroys all the values of solidarity and humanity, and sometimes produces direct violence. Those who deplore the cynicism of the men and women of our time should not omit to relate it to the economic and social conditions which favour or demand it and which reward it.

So insecurity acts directly on those it touches (and whom it renders incapable of mobilizing themselves) and indirectly on all the others, through the fear it arouses, which is methodically exploited by all the *insecurity-inducing strategies*, such as the introduction of the notorious 'flexibility', – which , it will have become clear, is inspired as much by political as economic reasons. One thus begins to suspect that insecurity is the product not of an *economic inevitability*, identified with the much-heralded 'globalization', but of a *political will*. A 'flexible' company in a sense deliberately exploits a situation of insecurity which it helps to reinforce: it seeks to reduce its costs, but also to make this lowering possible by putting the workers in permanent danger of losing their jobs. The whole world of production, material and cultural, public and private, is thus carried along by a process of intensification of insecurity, with, for example, the *deterritorialization* of the company. An industry previously linked to a nation-state or a region (Detroit or Turin for automobiles) tends increasingly to detach itself through what is called the 'network corporation', organized on a continental or world scale and linking production segments,

technological know-how, communication networks and training facilities scattered between very distant places.

By facilitating or organizing the mobility of capital and
'delocalization' towards the countries with the lowest wages,
neo-liberal policies have helped to extend competition among
workers to a global level. The national (and perhaps national-
ized) company, whose field of competition was more or less
strictly limited to the national territory, and which went out to
win markets abroad, has given way to the multinational
corporation which places workers in competition no longer just
with their compatriots or even, as the demagogues claim, with
the foreigners installed on the national territory, who are in fact
clearly the first victims of loss of security, but with workers on
the other side of the world, who are forced to accept poverty-
line wages.

Casualization of employment is part of a *mode of domination*
of a new kind, based on the creation of a generalized and
permanent state of insecurity aimed at forcing workers into
submission, into the acceptance of exploitation. To characterize
this mode of domination, which, although in its effects it closely
resembles the wild capitalism of the early days, is entirely
unprecedented, a speaker here proposed the very appropriate
and expressive concept of *flexploitation*. The word evokes very
well this rational management of insecurity which, especially
through the concerted manipulation of the space of production,
sets up competition between the workers of the countries with
the greatest social gains and the best organized union resistance
– features that are linked to a national territory and history –
and the workers of the socially least advanced countries, and so
breaks resistance and obtains obedience and submission, through
apparently natural mechanisms which thus serve as their own
justification. These submissive dispositions produced by insecur-

ity are the prerequisite for an increasingly 'successful' exploitation, based on the division between the growing number who
do not work and the diminishing number of those who work, but
who work more and more. So it seems to me that what is
presented as an economic system governed by the iron laws of
a kind of social nature is in reality a *political system* which can
only be set up with the active or passive complicity of the
officially political powers.

Against this political system, political struggle is possible. In
the form of charitable or militant activity, it can first aim to
encourage the victims of exploitation, all the present and
potential victims of insecurity, to work together against the
destructive effects of insecurity (by helping them to live, to
'hold on', to save their dignity, to resist destructuring, loss of
self-respect, alienation) and above all to mobilize *on an
international scale*, that is to say at the same level at which the
policy of inducing insecurity exerts its effects, so as to combat
this policy and neutralize the competition it seeks to create
between the workers of different countries. But it can also try
to help workers to break away from the logic of past struggles
which, being based on the demand for work and for better pay
for work, trap them within work and within the exploitation (or
flexploitation) which accompanies it. This implies a redistribu-
tion of work (through a significant reduction in the working
week throughout Europe), inseparable from a redefinition of the
distribution between production time and reproduction time,
rest and leisure.

This revolution would have to start with the abandonment
of the narrowly calculating and individualistic view which
reduces agents to calculators concerned with resolving problems, strictly economic problems in the narrowest sense of the
word. In order for the economic system to function, the workers

have to bring into it their own conditions of production and reproduction, but also what is needed for the economic system itself to function, starting with their belief in the company, in work, in the necessity of work, and so on. These are all things that the orthodox economists exclude *a priori* from their abstract and partial accountancy, tacitly leaving the responsibility for the production and reproduction of all the hidden economic and social requirements for the economy as they know it to individuals or, paradoxically, to the state, of which they otherwise urge the destruction.

Grenoble, December 1997

Notes

1 Bourdieu, *Travail et travailleurs en Algérie*; Bourdieu, *Algeria 1960*.

The Protest Movement of the Unemployed, a Social Miracle

This movement of the unemployed is a unique, extraordinary event. Contrary to what we are told, day in, day out, on television and in the newspapers, this *French exception* is something we can be proud of. All the research on unemployment has shown that it destroys its victims, wiping out their defences and their subversive dispositions. If that inevitability has been overturned, it is thanks to the tireless work of individuals and associations which have encouraged, supported and organized the movement. I cannot help finding it extraordinary that left-wing politicians or trade unionists talk of manipulation (in the same terms in which nineteenth-century employers denounced the early trade unions) where they ought to recognize the virtues of the work of activists, without which, it is clear, there would never have been anything resembling a social movement. For my part, I want to express my admiration and gratitude – all the greater because what they were taking on often seemed to me hopeless – for all those, in the unions and

Remarks on 17 Jan. 1998, at the time of the occupation of the École Normale Supérieure by the unemployed.

associations brought together in the États Généraux du Mouvement Social, who have made possible what is truly a *social miracle*, the virtues and benefits of which will be long-lasting.

The first conquest of this movement is the movement itself, its very existence: it pulls the unemployed, and with them all insecure workers, whose number increases daily, out of invisibility, isolation, silence, in short, out of non-existence. Re-emerging into the light of day, the unemployed give back their existence and some pride in themselves to all the men and women that non-employment consigns, like them, to oblivion and shame. Above all they remind us that one of the foundations of the present economic and social order is mass unemployment and the threat this implies for all those who still have a job. Far from being wrapped up in an egoistic movement, they are saying that even if no unemployed person is quite like another, the differences between people on welfare-to-work schemes, the unemployed whose benefits have expired or those receiving specific allowances, are not radically different from those between the unemployed and all insecure workers. This is a reality which tends to be masked and forgotten when the emphasis is put on the (so to speak) 'sectional' claims of the unemployed, which are liable to separate them from the employed, especially those in the most insecure positions, who may feel forgotten.

Moreover, unemployment and the unemployed haunt work and the worker. Short-term, part-time and temporary workers of every category, in industry, commerce, education, entertainment, even if there are immense differences between them and the unemployed and also between themselves, all live in fear of unemployment and, very often, under the threat of the blackmail that can be used against them. Instability of employment opens up new strategies of domination and exploitation, based on intimidation through the threat of redundancy, which occurs now at all levels of the hierarchy, in private and even public enterprises and which subjects the whole world of work, especially those in the cultural sector, to a crushing censorship that forbids mobilization and takes away bargaining power. The generalized worsening of working conditions is made possible or even favoured by unemployment and it is because they are obscurely aware of this that so many French people feel and express solidarity with the struggle of the unemployed. That is why it is possible to say, without playing with words, that the mobilization of those whose existence is undoubtedly the main factor in a loss of militancy is the most extraordinary encouragement to mobilization, to the rejection of political fatalism.

The movement of the French unemployed is also a call to all the unemployed and all the casualized workers of the whole of Europe: a new subversive idea has appeared on the scene, and it can become an instrument of struggle available to every national movement. The unemployed are reminding all workers that their interests are bound up with those of the unemployed; that the unemployed whose existence weighs so heavily on them and on their working conditions are the product of a policy; that a mobilization capable of overcoming the frontiers that exist, in every country, between workers and non-workers and the frontiers between all the workers and non-workers of one country and the workers and non-workers of every other country could counter the policy which can mean that the non-workers can force silence and resignation on those who have the dubious 'privilege' of a more or less precarious employment.

Paris, January 1998

The Negative Intellectual

All those who have been there, day after day, year after year, to receive Algerian refugees, to listen to them, help them draw up a curriculum vitae and go through the formalities in the ministries, to accompany them to court, to write letters to the authorities, to go in delegations to see officials, to apply for visas, authorizations and residence permits, who were mobilized, as soon as the first murders started in June 1993, not only to provide help and protection so far as was possible, but to try to inform themselves and inform others, to understand and explain a complex reality, who have fought tirelessly, through public declarations, press conferences and newspaper articles, to rescue the Algerian crisis from one-sided interpretations, all the intellectuals of all countries who have come together to fight indifference or xenophobia, to reinstate respect for the complexity of the world by untangling the confusions that some people deliberately maintain, have suddenly discovered that all their efforts could be undone, swept away, in two strokes, three movements.

This text was written in January 1998; it is published for the first time in this volume.

Two articles[1] written after a journey planned, mapped out, escorted and watched over by the Algerian authorities or army, and published in the most respected French newspaper, though full of platitudes and errors and entirely oriented towards a simplistic conclusion calculated to give satisfaction to superficial pity and racist hatred, masked as humanist indignation; a unanimist public meeting bringing together the cream of the media intelligentsia and the political class, from the fundamentalist liberal and the opportunist ecologist to the passionaria of the 'eradicators';[2] a television programme which is entirely one-sided under the appearance of neutrality – and the trick is pulled off. Everything is back to zero. The negative intellectual has done his job: who could want to express solidarity with mass murderers and rapists – especially when they are people who are described, without historical justification, as 'madmen of Islam', enveloped under the abominated name of Islamicism, the quintessence of all Oriental fanaticism, designed to give racist contempt the impeccable alibi of ethical and secular legitimacy?

To pose the problem in such terms, you don't need to be a great intellectual. And yet that is how the originator of this crude operation of symbolic policing, which is the absolute antithesis of everything that defines the intellectual – freedom with respect to those in power, the critique of received ideas, the demolition of simplistic either-ors, respect for the complexity of problems – has come to be consecrated by journalists as an intellectual in the full sense of the word.

And yet I know all kinds of people who, though they know all that very well, because they have grappled countless times with those forces, will start again, each in their own way and with their own means, on work that is always liable to be destroyed by a thoughtless, frivolous or malicious article or to be annexed, if it succeeds, by opportunists and eleventh-hour converts; who will persist in writing corrections, refutations and rebuttals destined to be overwhelmed by the uninterrupted flow of media chatter, because they are convinced that – as we have seen from the movement of the unemployed, the fruition of obscure efforts, sometimes so desperate that they seem to be the art for art's sake of politics – one can, in the long run, give a push to the rock of Sisyphus without it rolling back.

They do so because, meanwhile, politicians who are skilled in neutralizing the social movements that have brought them to power continue to leave thousands of 'unauthorized' immigrants without an answer or to deport them to the country from which they have fled, which could be Algeria.

Paris, January 1998

Notes

1 By Bernard Henri-Lévy, in *Le Monde* (trans.).
2 This is a reference to Khalida Messaoudi, co-author (with Elisabeth Schemla) of *Une Algérienne debout: entretiens* (Paris, Flammarion, 1995) (trans.).

Neo-liberalism, the Utopia (Becoming a Reality) of Unlimited Exploitation

Is the economic world really, as the dominant discourse would have us believe, a pure and perfect order, implacably unfolding the logic of its predictable consequences and promptly repressing all deviations from its rules through the sanctions it inflicts, either automatically or, more exceptionally, through its armed agent, the IMF or the OECD and the drastic policies they impose – reduced labour costs, cuts in public spending and a more 'flexible' labour market? What if it were, in reality, only the implementation of a utopia, neo-liberalism, thus converted into a *political programme*, but a utopia which, with the aid of the economic theory to which it subscribes, manages to see itself as the scientific description of reality?

This tutelary theory is a pure mathematical fiction, based, from the outset, on a gigantic abstraction, which, contrary to what economists who defend their right to inevitable abstraction like to think, cannot be reduced to the effect – constitutive of every scientific project – of object construction as a deliberately selective apprehension of the real. This abstraction, performed in the name of a strict and narrow view of rationality, identified with individual rationality, consists in bracketing off the economic and social conditions of rational dispositions (and in particular those of the calculating disposition applied to economic matters which is the basis of the neo-liberal view) and of the economic and social structures which are the condition of their exercise, or, more precisely, of the production and reproduction of those dispositions and those structures. To appreciate the scale of the omission, one only has to think of the educational system, which is never taken into account *as such* at a time when it plays a decisive role both in the production of goods and services and in the production of producers. From this original fault, inscribed in the Walrasian[1] myth of 'pure theory', flow all the omissions and shortcomings of the discipline of economics, and the deadly stubbornness with which it clings to the arbitrary opposition it causes to exist, by its very existence, between specifically economic logic – based on competition and promising efficiency – and social logic, subject to the rule of equity.

Having said this, this initially desocialized and dehistoricized 'theory' has, now more than ever, the means of *making itself true*, empirically falsifiable. For neo-liberal discourse is not a discourse like others. Like psychiatric discourse in the asylum, as described by Erving Goffman,[2] it is a 'strong discourse' which is so strong and so hard to fight because it has behind it all the powers of a world of power relations which it helps to make as it is, in particular by orienting the economic choices of those who dominate economic relations and so adding its own – specifically symbolic – force to those power relations. In the name of the scientific programme of knowledge, converted into a political programme of action, an immense *political operation* is being pursued (denied, because it is apparently purely negative), aimed at creating the conditions for realizing and operating of the 'theory'; a *programme of methodical destruction of collectives* (neo-classical economics recognizes only individuals, whether it is dealing with companies, trade unions or families).

The movement, made possible by the policy of financial deregulation, towards the neo-liberal utopia of a pure, perfect market takes place through the transforming and, it has to be said, *destructive* action of all the political measures (the most recent being the MAI, the Multilateral Agreement on Investment, intended to protect foreign companies and their investments against national governments) aimed at *putting into question all the collective structures* capable of obstructing the logic of the pure market: the nation-state, whose room for manoeuvre is steadily shrinking; work groups, with for example the individualization of salaries and careers on the basis of individual performance and the consequent atomization of workers; collectives defending workers' rights – unions, societies and cooperatives; even the family, which, through the segmentation of the market into age groups, loses some of its control over consumption. Deriving its social force from the political and economic strength of those whose interests it defends – shareholders, financial operators, industrialists, conservative politicians or social democrats converted to the cosy capitulations of laissez-faire, senior officials of the financial ministries, who are all the more determined to impose a policy implying their own redundancy because, unlike private-sector executives, they run no risk of suffering the consequences – the neo-liberal programme tends overall to favour the separation between the economy and social realities and so to construct, in reality, an economic system corresponding to the theoretical description, in other words a kind of logical machine, which presents itself as a chain of constraints impelling the economic agents.

The globalization of financial markets, combined with the progress of information technology, ensures an unprecedented mobility of capital and gives investors (or shareholders) concerned about their immediate interests, that is the short-term profitability of their investments, the possibility of continuously comparing the profitability of the largest companies and appropriately sanctioning relative failure. Companies themselves, exposed to this permanent threat, have to adjust ever more rapidly to the demands of the markets, for fear of 'losing the confidence of the markets' and with it the support of shareholders who, with their eyes fixed on short-term profitability, are increasingly able to impose their will on the managers, to lay down guidelines for them, through the finance departments, and to shape their policies on recruitment, employment and wages. This leads to the absolute reign of flexibility, with recruitment on short-term contracts or on a temporary basis and repeated 'downsizing', and the creation, within the company itself, of competition between autonomous 'profit centres', between teams, forced into providing all their own services, and finally, between individuals, through the individualization of the wage relation. This comes through the setting of individual objectives; individual appraisal interviews; personal increments or bonuses based on individual competence or merit; individualized career paths; strategies of 'responsibilization' tending to secure the self-exploitation of some managers who, while remaining wage-earners subject to strong hierarchical authority, are at the same time held responsible for their sales, their products, their branch, their shop, etc., like 'independent' proprietors; the demand for 'self-appraisal' which extends the 'involvement' of employees, in accordance with the techniques of 'participatory management', far beyond the executive level – all methods of rational control which, while imposing over-investment in work, and not only in posts of responsibility, and work under the pressures of urgency, combine to weaken or destroy collective references and solidarity.[3]

The practical instituting of a Darwinian world in which the springs of commitment to the job and the company are found in insecurity, suffering and stress[4] would undoubtedly not succeed so completely if it did not benefit from the complicity of the destabilized habitus produced by insecurity and the existence – at all levels of the hierarchy, even the highest, especially among executives – of a reserve army of labour made docile by insecure employment and the permanent threat of unemployment. The ultimate basis of this economic order placed under the banner of individual freedom is indeed the *structural violence* of unemployment, of insecure employment and of the *fear* provoked by the threat of losing employment. The condition of the 'harmonious' functioning of the individualist micro-economic model and the principle of individual 'motivation' at work lie, in the final analysis, in a mass phenomenon, the existence of the reserve army of the unemployed – though the term 'army' is inappropriate, because unemployment isolates, atomizes, individualizes, demobilizes and strips away solidarity.

This structural violence also bears on what is called the work contract (wilfully rationalized and derealized by the 'theory of contracts'). Corporate discourse has never spoken so much about trust, cooperation, loyalty and corporate culture as now when the worker's unremitting commitment is obtained by sweeping away all temporal guarantees (three-quarters of new hirings are on short-term contracts, the proportion of insecure jobs rises steadily, restrictions on individual redundancies are being removed). This commitment is, moreover, necessarily uncertain and ambiguous, since casualization, fear of redundancy, downsizing can, like unemployment, generate anxiety, demoralization or conformism (faults which the managerial literature identifies and deplores). In this world without inertia, without an immanent principle of continuity, those at the bottom are like the creatures in a Cartesian universe: they hang on the arbitrary decision of a power responsible for the 'continued creation' of their existence – as is shown and confirmed by the threat of plant closure, disinvestment and relocation.

The particular character of the profound sense of insecurity and uncertainty about themselves and their future which affects all workers exposed to casualization stems from the fact that the principle of the division between those who are thrown back into the reserve army and those who are kept in work lies in *academically guaranteed competence*, which is also the basis of the division, within the 'technically advanced' company, between the executives or 'technicians' and the production-line workers, the new pariahs of industrial society. The generalization of electronics, IT and quality standards, which requires all wage-earners to retrain and perpetuates the equivalent of school tests within the enterprise, tends to reinforce the sense of insecurity with a sense of *unworthiness*, deliberately fostered by the hierarchy. The occupational world, and by extension the whole social world, seems based on a ranking by 'competence', or, worse, of 'intelligence'. More, perhaps, than technical manipulations of working relations and the strategies especially designed to obtain the submission and obedience which are the focus of constant attention and permanent reinvention, more than the enormous investment in staff, time, research and work that is presupposed by the constant reinvention of new forms of 'human resource' management, it is the belief in the hierarchy of academically guaranteed competences which underlies order and discipline in private companies and also, increasingly, in the public sector. Manual workers – condemned to job insecurity and threatened with relegation into the indignity of unemployment, forced to define themselves in relation to the great nobility from the top-rank schools, destined for the command posts, and to the lesser nobility of clerks and technicians, who are assigned to tasks of implementation and always on sufferance because they are permanently required to *prove themselves* – can only form a disenchanted image both of themselves and of their group. Once an object of pride, rooted in traditions and sustained by a whole technical and political heritage, manual workers as a group – if indeed it still exists as such – are thrown into demoralization, devaluation and political disillusionment, which is expressed in the crisis of activism or, worse, in a desperate rallying to the themes of quasi-fascist extremism.

It can be seen how the neo-liberal utopia tends to be embodied in the reality of a kind of infernal machine, its necessity felt even by the dominant themselves – sometimes troubled, like George Soros, or the occasional pension fund manager, by anxiety at the destructive effects of the power they wield and led into compensatory actions inspired by the very logic that they want to neutralize, as with the benefactions of a Bill Gates. Like Marxism in earlier times, with which, in this respect, it has many common features, this utopia generates a potent belief, 'free trade faith', not only among those who live from it materially such as financiers, big businessmen, etc., but also those who derive from it their justifications for existing, such as the senior civil servants and politicians who deify the power of the markets in the name of economic efficiency, who demand the lifting of the administrative or political barriers that could hinder the owners of capital in their purely individual pursuit of maximum individual profit instituted as a model of rationality, who want independent central banks, who preach the subordination of the national states to the demands of economic freedom for the masters of the economy, with the suppression of all regulations on all markets, starting with the labour market, the forbidding of deficits and inflation, general-ized privatization of public services, and the reduction of public and welfare spending.

Without necessarily sharing the economic and social interests of the true believers, economists have sufficient specific interests in the field of economic science to make a decisive contribution, whatever their emotional responses to the economic and social effects of the utopia that they dress up in mathematical reason, to the production and reproduction of the neo-liberal utopia. Cut off by their whole existence and above all by their generally purely abstract and theoretical intellectual training from the real economic and social world, they are, like others in other times in the field of philosophy, particularly inclined to take the things of logic for the logic of things. Trusting in models that they have practically never had the occasion to subject to experimental verification, tending to look down from on high on the conclu-sions of the other historical sciences, in which they recognize only the purity and crystalline transparency of their mathematical games and whose real necessity and deep complexity they are most often unable to comprehend, they participate and collabor-ate in an enormous economic and social transformation which, even if some of its consequences horrify them (they may subscribe to the Socialist Party and give considered advice to its representatives in the highest decision-making bodies), cannot entirely displease them, since, with a few 'blips', mainly attrib-utable to what they call 'speculative fevers', it tends to give reality to the ultra-consistent utopia (like some forms of lunacy) to which they devote their lives.

And yet, the world is there, with the immediately visible effects of the implementation of the great neo-liberal utopia: not only the poverty and suffering of a growing proportion of the population of the economically most advanced societies, the extraordinary growth in disparities in incomes, the progressive disappearance of the autonomous worlds of cultural production, cinema, publishing, etc., and therefore, ultimately, of cultural products themselves, because of the growing intrusion of commercial considerations, but also and above all the destruction of all the collective institutions capable of standing up to the effects of the infernal machine – in the forefront of which is the state, the repository of all the universal ideas associated with the idea of the *public* – and the imposition, everywhere, at the highest levels of the economy and the state, or in corporations, of that kind of moral Darwinism which, with the cult of the 'winner', establishes the struggle of all against all and *cynicism* as the norm of all practices. And the new moral order, based on the reversal of all sets of values, is displayed in the spectacle, calmly diffused in the media, of all those high representatives of the state who abase the dignity of their position by bowing before the bosses of multinationals, Daewoo or Toyota, or competing to charm Bill Gates with their smiles and gestures of complicity.

Is it reasonable to expect that the extraordinary mass of suffering produced by such a political and economic regime could one day give rise to a movement capable of stopping the rush into the abyss? In fact, we see here an extraordinary paradox: on the one hand, the obstacles encountered on the route to the new order, that of the individual who is solitary, but free, are now seen as attributable to rigidities or archaisms, and any direct or conscious intervention, at least when it comes from the state, through whatever channel, is discredited in advance on the grounds that it is inspired by civil servants pursuing their own interests and oblivious to the interests of the economic agents and it is therefore suggested that that intervention be withdrawn in favour of a pure, anonymous mechanism, the market (which people forget is also the realm of the exercise of interests); yet on the other hand, it is in reality the permanence or the survival of institutions and agents of the old order now being dismantled, and all the work of the different kinds of 'social workers', and also all social, familial and other solidarities, which prevent the social order from collapsing into chaos in spite of the growing volume of the population cast into insecurity. The transition to 'liberalism' takes place imperceptibly, like continental drift, concealing its most terrible long-term effects. These effects are thus masked, paradoxically, by the resistances it arouses, even now, from those who defend the old order by drawing on the resources stored up in it, in the legal or practical models of assistance and solidarity that it offered, in the habitus it favoured (among nurses, social workers, etc.), in short, in the reserves of social capital which protect a whole block of the present social order from falling into anomie (a capital which, if it is not renewed, reproduced, will inevitably run out, but which is still far from exhaustion).

But these same forces of 'conservation', which it is too facile to treat as conservative forces, are also, in another respect, forces of *resistance* to the establishment of the new order, which can become subversive forces – so long as we know how to conduct the symbolic struggle against the incessant work of the neo-liberal 'thinkers' aimed at discrediting and disqualifying the heritage of words, traditions and representations associated with the historical conquests of the social movements of the past and the present; on condition, too, that we know how to defend the corresponding institutions, labour law, social welfare, social security, etc., against the endeavour to consign them to the archaism of an outmoded past or, worse, to redefine them perversely as unnecessary and unacceptable privileges. This is not an easy battle and it is not uncommon to have to fight it in the opposite terms. Inspired by a paradoxical intention of *subversion oriented towards conservation or restoration*, the revolutionary conservatives find it easy to define as reactionary resistances the defensive reactions provoked by the conservative actions they describe as revolutionary; and to condemn as the archaic and retrograde defence of 'privileges' demands and revolts that appeal to established rights, in other words to a past threatened with deterioration or destruction by their regressive measures – the clearest example being the sacking of trade union representatives or, more radically, of the oldest workers, the trustees of the traditions of the group.

And so if one can retain some reasonable hope, it is that, in state institutions and also in the dispositions of agents (especially those most attached to these institutions, like the minor state nobility), there still exist forces which, under the appearance of simply defending a vanishing order and the corresponding 'privileges' (which is what they will be accused of), will in fact, to withstand the pressure, have to work to invent and construct a social order which is not governed solely by the pursuit of selfish interest and individual profit, and which makes room for collectives oriented towards *rational pursuit of collectively defined and approved ends*. Among these collectives – associations, unions and parties – a special place should surely be made for the state, national or, better still, supranational, in other words a European state (as a stage on the way to a world state), capable of effectively controlling and taxing the profits made on the financial markets; capable also, and above all, of countering the destructive action which these markets exert on the labour market, by organizing, with the aid of the unions, the definition and defence of the *public interest* – which, whether one likes it or not, will never, even by juggling the figures, be produced by the accountant's view of the world (once one would have said 'grocer's') which the new belief presents as the supreme form of human achievement.

Paris, January 1998

Notes

1 August Walras (1800–66), French economist, was one of the first to attempt to apply mathematics to the study of economics (trans.).
2 E. Goffman, *Asylums*.
3 On all these matters, see the two issues of *Actes de la Recherche en Sciences Sociales* devoted to 'The new forms of domination at work' (114, Sept. 1996, and 115, Dec. 1996), and especially the introduction by Gabrielle Balazs and Michel Pialoux, 'Crise du travail et crise du politique' (114, pp. 3–4).
4 Dejours, *Souffrance en France*.

References

The list includes cited references and related works.

Accardo, A. et al., *Journalistes au quotidien: outils pour une socioanalyse des pratiques journalistiques*, Bordeaux: Le Mascaret, 1995.

Actes de la Recherche en Sciences Sociales , 'L'économie de la maison', 81–2, Mar. 1990.

——'La souffrance', 90, Dec. 1991.

——'Les nouvelles formes de domination au travail', 114, Sept. 1996, and 115, Dec. 1996.

——'Histoire de l'État', 116–17, Mar. 1997.

——'Les ruses de la raison impérialiste', 121–2, Mar. 1998.

Bloch, E., *L'Esprit de l'utopie*, Paris: Gallimard, 1977.

Boschetti, A., *Sartre et* Les Temps Modernes*: une entreprise intellectuelle*, Paris: Minuit, 1976.

Bourdieu, P., *Travail et travailleurs en Algérie*, Paris and The Hague: Mouton, 1963 (with A. Darbel, J. P. Rivet and C. Seibel).

——*Algeria 1960*, Cambridge: Cambridge University Press, 1979.

——'Deux impérialismes de l'universel', in C. Fauré and T.

Bishop (eds), *L'Amérique des Français*, Paris: Éditions François Bourin, 1992.

——'The racism of intelligence', in *Sociology in Question*, London: Sage, 1993.

——*The State Nobility: Elite Schools in the Field of Power*, Cambridge: Polity Press, 1996.

——*Méditations pascaliennes*, Paris: Seuil, 1997.

Bourdieu, P. et al., *La Misère du monde*, Paris: Seuil, 1993.

Champagne, P., *Faire l'opinion*, Paris: Minuit, 1993.

——'Le journalisme entre précarité et concurrence', *Liber*, 29, Dec. 1996.

Charle, C., *Naissance des intellectuels*, Paris: Minuit, 1990.

Dejours, C., *Souffrance en France: la banalisation de l'injustice sociale*, Paris: Seuil, 1997.

Dezalay, Y. and B. B. Garth, *Dealing in Virtue*, Chicago: Chicago University Press, 1995.

Dezalay, Y. and D. Sugarman, *Professional Competition Power: Lawyers, Accountants and the Social Construction of Markets*, London and New York: Routledge, 1995.

Dixon, K., 'Les Evangélistes du Marché', *Liber*, 32, Sept. 1997, pp. 5–6.

Fallows, J., *Breaking the News: How Media Undermine American Democracy*, New York: Vintage Books, 1997.

Ferry, L. and A. Renaut, *La Pensée 68*, Paris: Gallimard, 1985.

Goffman, E., *Asylums: Essays on the Social Situation of Mental Patients and Other Inmates*, Harmondsworth: Penguin, 1961.

Grémion, P., *Preuves, une revue européenne à Paris*, Paris: Julliard, 1989.

——*Intelligence de l'anti-communisme: le congrès pour la liberté de la culture à Paris*, Paris: Fayard, 1995.

Halimi, S., *Les Nouveaux Chiens de garde*, Paris: Liber–Raisons d'Agir, 1997.

Liber, 'Mouvements divers: le choix de la subversion', 33, Dec. 1997.

Pasche, C. and S. Peters, 'Les premiers pas de la Société du Mont-Pélerin ou les dessous chics du néolibéralisme', *Les Annuelles* (L'avènement des sciences sociales comme disciplines académiques), 8, 1997, pp. 191–216.

Salesse, Y., *Propositions pour une autre Europe: construire Babel*, Paris: Félin, 1997.

Théret, B., *L'État, la finance et le social*, Paris: La Découverte, 1995.

Vidal-Naquet, P., *Les Juifs, la mémoire et le présent*, Paris: La Découverte, vol. 1 1981, vol. 2 1991.

Wacquant, L., 'De l'État charitable à l'État pénal: notes sur le traitement politique de la misère en Amérique', *Regards Sociologiques*, 11, 1996.

Printed in the USA
CPSIA information can be obtained
at www.ICGtesting.com
LVHW010851080824
787594LV00002B/108